About the Author

Susan Singleton is a solicitor with her own London firm, Singletons, which specialises in competition law, intellectual property law, IT/ecommerce and general commercial law. Articled at Nabarro Nathanson, she joined Slaughter and May's EC/Competition Law Department on qualifying in 1985, moving to Bristows in March 1988, where she remained until founding her own firm in 1994. Since then she has advised over 480 clients. According to the Chambers and Partners Legal Directory she is one of the UK's leading IT lawyers. In 2002 she acted for the claimant in the first damages action for breach of the EU competition rules to come before the English courts, *Arkin v Borchard and Others*. Her clients range from major plcs and institutions to small start-up businesses.

She is author of over 30 law books on topics such as internet and ecommerce law, competition law, commercial agency law, data protection legislation and intellectual property, and writes fifteen legal articles a month. She is a frequent speaker in the intellectual property, competition and commercial law fields, both in the UK and abroad.

She is on the Committee of the Competition Law Association, is a member of the Licensing Executives Society (EC/Laws Committee) and serves on the Contracts Group of the Chartered Institute of Purchasing and Supply (CIPS) and is a member of the Society of Computers and Law and The Intellectual Property Lawyers' Organisation (TIPLO). She has five children and lives in London.

Singletons welcomes clients of any size.

Susan Singleton
Singletons
Solicitors
Tel 020 8866 1934
Fax 020 8866 5912
www.singlelaw.com
Email susan@singlelaw.com

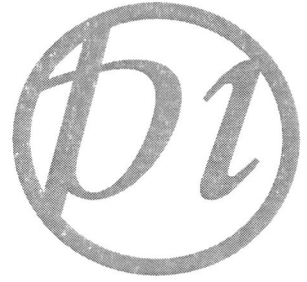

THOROGOOD
PROFESSIONAL
INSIGHTS

A SPECIALLY COMMISSIONED REPORT

THE FREEDOM OF INFORMATION ACT

Susan Singleton

THOROGOOD

Other Thorogood Professional Insights

Data Protection Act for Employers

Susan Singleton

Websites and the Law

Susan Singleton

Competition Act 1998:
Practical Advice

Susan Singleton

Applying the Employment Act 2002
– Crucial Developments for
Employers and Employees

Audrey Williams

HR Business Partners and
HR Outsourcing

Ian Hunter and Jane Saunders

Email – Legal Issues

Susan Singleton

Employee Sickness and
Fitness for Work

Gillian Howard

Special discounts for bulk quantities
of Thorogood books are available to
corporations, institutions, associations and
other organisations. For more information
contact Thorogood by telephone on
020 7749 4748, by fax on 020 7729 6110, or
email us: info@thorogood.ws

Thorogood Publishing Ltd
10-12 Rivington Street
London EC2A 3DU.

t: 020 7749 4748
f: 020 7729 6110
e: info@thorogood.ws
w: www.thorogood.ws

A CIP catalogue record for
this Report is available from
the British Library.

ISBN 1 85418 347 8

Printed in Great Britain
by printflow.com

Dedication

In memory of my mother, Anne Morgan who died 4th November 2004, whose love of information and thirst for knowledge lives on in her children. An inspired and inspiring teacher.

To my father, Dr Peter Morgan, whose zest for his work as a consultant psychiatrist kept him working full-time until his retirement in 2005, aged 76.

To my children, Rachel, Rebecca, Ben, Joseph and Sam. May you always live in an England free of censorship.

Contents

APPENDICES TO CHAPTER 2   24

3   EXEMPTIONS AND COMMERCIAL AND CONTRACT ISSUES   60

APPENDICES TO THIS REPORT   73

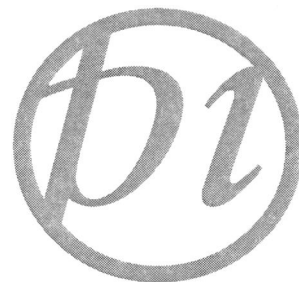

Chapter 1

Introduction

Chapter 1
Introduction

The Freedom of Information Act 2000 came into force on 1st January 2005 and gives companies and individuals important powers to request information from public bodies. This is the first point to note – it does not apply to information requests to private sector companies. However, the Data Protection Act 1998 does give individuals (not companies) rights to make a subject access request for details of information held about them by data controllers. DPA requests are limited to information relating to the individual. The FOIA is broader. However both should be considered where information is sought.

Journalists and politicians have found the FOIA particularly useful. Anyone involved in research will also find it potentially of use. This report in particular examines how businesses might find it useful and also possibly a risk to them if they have disclosed information to public bodies which is then disclosed by the public bodies once an FOIA request has been made.

The Act is policed by the Information Commissioner's Office. Information Commissioner Richard Thomas has received over 1,000 complaints (to July 2005) since the Freedom of Information Act came into force about alleged failures to comply with the Act. He has issued his 10 top tips for public authorities to avoid complaints.

10 Top Tips from the Information Commissioner's Office for Public Authorities

1. **Be positive**. Greater transparency is good for the public and democracy.

2. **Be active**. Use Publication Schemes pro-actively. Pro-active publication saves time, effort, resources and money.

3. **Anticipate requests** – don't wait to be asked.

4. **Why not?** The Act presumes disclosure. Public authorities should meet people's requests unless there is a good reason within the Act not to. Organisations do not have to withhold information if an exemption applies.

5. **Get talking**. A dialogue between the requester and the public authority can help you resolve requests more quickly.

6. **Don't fear precedent**. All decisions should be made on their own merits and on a case by case basis at the time of the request.

7. **Give clear reasons**. If you are turning down a request, write a clear Refusal Notice. Properly drafted and fully explained refusals can help avoid reviews and complaints.

8. **Give more if it helps**. Supply additional information where it is useful, such as an explanation of the data you are supplying.

9. **Meet it or beat it**. You must meet the 20 day deadline – beat it if possible.

10. **Help yourself**. Look at the ICO's guidance on http://www.ico.gov.uk/ for more information on freedom of information, as well as information on data protection, or you can ring the ICO's Helpline on 01625 545745.

Complaints

Where requests under the FOIA are not met then it is possible to make a complaint to the Information Commissioner. Most complaints over the handling of requests for information under the Act are being upheld based on the 14 decisions published to the date of writing. The Commissioner's Office only began publishing its decisions in July 2005. Of the 14 decisions to date, 11 complaints (or 79%) were upheld, at least in part. The public authorities are simply told just to provide the information requested.

Effects

A briefing in 2005 from the Society of Information Technology Management (Socitm) says that the FOIA should be regarded as making a positive contribution to the establishment of best practice in the management of information within local authorities and other public services. The briefing is intended to remind managers that the requirements of FOI "demand detailed thinking about a wide range of information management issues".

Examples include the need for organisations to know what information they hold, whether it is accurate and up-to-date, where such information can be found,

whether it is exempt from publication under FOI and the extent to which the organisation can be open with its information.

Freedom of Information: 4,000 requests in the first month

The Information Commissioner's Office has published a guide on how to complain if information requested under the Freedom of Information Act has not been disclosed. There were 4,000 requests in the first month that the Act was in force. The new guide, *'Your right to know: how to complain'*, gives details on the complaints procedure, the information needed by the Information Commissioner's Office (ICO) and the powers given to the ICO to obtain the information requested. About half of the first 4,000 requests have been made by reporters, with most requests (over 600) being made to the National Archives. The Ministry of Defence and the Foreign and Commonwealth Office were also top targets, and typical requests included applications for information about artwork loaned from national collections to Cabinet Ministers' offices and official residences. The Department for Constitutional Affairs (DCA) received about 144 requests for information in January, 76 of those within the first three days of the Act coming into force. Of these early requests 55 have been answered, 19 are on target to be answered within the 20 working days.

In addition, local authorities have released information about a wide range of issues from pension schemes, car park contracts and repairs, to council buildings, to restaurant hygiene inspection reports and attacks on teachers in schools.

Case Example

Case Ref: FS50062329
Date: 12/07/05
Public Authority: Bridgnorth District Council

Summary: Following a complaint from a third party, the Council carried out an investigation into the state of a piece of land owned by the complainant to determine whether any enforcement action was appropriate under the Town & Country Planning Act 1990 (T&CP Act). The owner of the land requested the right to inspect the enforcement file. The Council originally dealt with the request under the FOI Act and refused it under

section 31 (2)(c) which relates to the prejudice of Regulatory activity. The Commissioner advised that the matter should be dealt with under the Environmental Information Regulations 2004. The Council subsequently claimed the information could be withheld under Regulation 12(5)(f) on the grounds that disclosure would adversely affect a criminal investigation. It is understood that the issuing of an enforcement notice under the T&CP Act is a civil sanction but failure to comply with such a notice is a criminal offence. However the Commissioner was not satisfied that an investigation to determine whether it was appropriate to issue an enforcement notice in the first place constituted an investigation of a criminal nature. Regarding the application of 12(5)(f), the ICO considered that in this case, the interests of the third party would only be adversely affected if their identity was revealed. The Decision Notice required the Council to provide access to all the information in the enforcement file apart from that which revealed the identity of the third party.

Section of Act/EIR & Finding:
EIR r.12(5)(b) – Upheld, EIR r.12(5)(f) – Upheld

Aims of this Report

This Report aims to provide guidance to those involved with FOIA in whatever manner. It is particularly directed at businesses who may need to grapple with the Act's provisions and need assistance in how to deal with the commercial issues which arise. It also aims to show readers where further information can be obtained on issues arising from the Act.

The Report principally deals with the laws of England and Wales. Scotland has its own information commissioner and reference should be made to the web site of that body at http://www.itspublicknowledge.info/

The Guide is up to date to 10 September 2005 and any errors and omissions are the author's own. Any comments can be directed to Susan Singleton at:
susan@singlelaw.com

Further information

- Information Commissioner's web site:
  www.informationcommissioner.gov.uk

- A large amount of detailed information is on the Department for
  Constitutional Affairs web site at:
  http://www.dca.gov.uk/majrepfr.htm#statdisc

- SOCITM FOIA briefing – The briefing costs £25 to non-members.
  See: http://www.socitm.gov.uk/Public/insight/orders/publications+.htm

- The ICO Guide can be ordered from the ICO by telephone on:
  08453 091091.

- The Scottish IC's office web site is:
  http://www.itspublicknowledge.info/

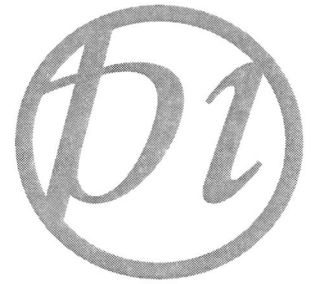

Chapter 2

The Freedom of Information
Act – Basics

Chapter 2

The Freedom of Information
Act – Basics

The Freedom of Information Act provides two ways for individuals and companies to obtain information held by public authorities:

Publication Schemes

The first such way is through a 'publication scheme' run by a public body. Readers should be able to find information about publication schemes run by public authorities by approaching that authority or looking on their web sites. The schemes are usually fairly similar in scope and set out how the information will be provided. A publication scheme is a public commitment to make certain information available and a guide to how that information can be obtained.

Contents of a Scheme

A Scheme is not a list of publications or of documents. It is simply a guide to what is available. There is no standard list of what must be included in a Scheme, but the sorts of information one can expect to find include:

- All the information the Authority is required to publish by law.

- Information about decisions made by the Authority and the reasons for those decisions.

- Information which the Authority thinks will be of general interest or which will help the public to better understand its role.

General Right of Access

Since 1st January 2005 there has been a general right of access to information held by public authorities whether they have a publication scheme or not. This is the second method by which to obtain information.

Exemptions

A very important part of the Act is the list of exemptions that there are from the Act, which are addressed in the next chapter. The Act also sets out procedures for dealing with requests, for example, time limits and fee, that can be charged for dealing with a request and so on.

Complaints

The Information Commissioner is the independent regulator for the Act with responsibilities to promote the Act and enforce compliance with its provisions. These powers include to make decisions as to whether a public authority has dealt with requests properly. As mentioned in Chapter 1 from July 2005 such decisions began to be published.

Case Examples

1. Case Ref: FAC0066292
Date: 12/07/05
Public Authority: The Home Office

Summary: The complainant requested information relating to Nazi war criminals living in the UK. The Home Office failed to respond to the complainant's request for information within the statutory time period but subsequently issued a satisfactory Refusal Notice. The Decision Notice identified the breach but no further steps were required. **Section of Act/EIR & Finding: FOI s.10 – Upheld**

2. Case Ref: FS50074330
Date: 05/07/05
Public Authority: Chorley Borough Council

Summary: The complainant requested information relating to the incidence of road traffic accidents. The Council failed to respond within the statutory time period but subsequently provided the information. Therefore, the Decision Notice identified the breach but no further steps were required. **Section of Act/EIR & Finding: FOI s.10 – Upheld**

Public authority?

The Act applies to public authorities. There are about 100,000 of these in the UK.

A 'public authority' is defined as any body which is:

   i)   Listed in Schedule 1 (of the FOIA); or

   ii)   Designated by order under section 5 (in the form of commencement orders, passed since the Act received royal assent); or

   iii) A publicly-owned company as defined by section 6.

Public authorities include:

- Central Government Departments and Agencies

- Local Government

- Police

- NHS

- State schools, colleges and universities

- Publicly owned companies

Information held on behalf of a third party

For the purposes of the Act, information is held by a public authority if:

   a)   it is held by the authority, otherwise than on behalf of another person, or

   b)   it is held by another person on behalf of the authority.

All information created by a public authority will be caught by the Act. The IC's office Awareness Guidance 12 says:

"An example of where a third party might hold information on behalf of a public authority is a Parish Council whose records are held by the local District Authority. This information would still be 'held' by the Parish Council for the purposes of the Act and the Parish Council would therefore have to deal with requests for this information accord to the requirements of the Act."

County councils often hold records that belong to district councils and universities will hold information on behalf of companies which they have established in order to exploit commercial research. The IC says:

> "As this information belongs to a public authority it will be subject to the provisions of the Act. However, you will not be required to provide this information in response to requests as it is the originating public authority that will 'hold' it for the purposes of the Act. Instead, you should:
>
> a) Ask the applicant to re-direct their request to the originating public authority; or
>
> b) Transfer the request to the originating authority; or
>
> c) Deal with the request yourself, but consult with the originating authority, whose responsibility it is to make the disclosure decision, in case they believe that some/all of the information could be exempt from disclosure under the Act."

If information is permanently given to a public authority it is also caught. For example Churchill might have left his papers to the nation. Some people give information in lieu of tax. The IC says such information would only be exempt if it fell within an exemption(s) provided by the Act.

Read-only information

If a public authority just has read only access to information such as where a central electronic repository containing information created by a number of public authorities allows them to read but not change it. Each public authority would be able to access each other's information from it but on a read-only basis.

The IC says:

> "In this case, it is the public authority which created the information and provided it to the repository that 'holds' it for the purposes of FOI. This means that if a public authority receives a request for information located in the repository that it has not created, it should at the very least refer the applicant to the authority that 'holds' the information. However, public authorities are under a duty to provide reasonable advice and assistance to applicants. If an authority is confident that the information requested and to which it has read-only access is not exempt, and it would be as easy to provide a copy of the information as to redirect the applicant, then it would be good practice to provide a copy."

The Awareness Guide 12 also looks at public records that have been transferred to a Public Record Office (or another place of deposit appointed by the Lord Chancellor). Are they still 'held' by the public authority? The IC does not think so as they are then held by the Public Record Office. So if the public authority received a request for a transferred record, the public authority would be under a duty to inform the applicant that it is no longer held by them and provide the applicant with the appropriate advice and assistance that would enable them to redirect their request as appropriate.

Private information

Some private information is held by public authorities. The Department for Work and Pensions holds private information in connection with social security claims. Public Record Offices and libraries may hold private information which has been loaned to them if they consider that information to be of public interest. For example, an individual may loan his family archives to a library in order for them to be viewed by the public. A further example of private information that is caught by the Act is comments received by a public authority from a private individual that relates to a consultation exercise conducted by that public authority.

In these circumstances the public authority will have an interest in this information and will make disclosure decisions. This is because although ownership rests with the depositor, the public authority with whom the information has been deposited effectively controls the information and holds it in its own right. It will therefore be difficult to argue that the information is merely held on behalf of another person and consequently not 'held' for the purposes of the public authority itself, the IC says. Those who have loaned material may in this case want to take it back if they are worried about FOIA requests being made in relation to it. They may also want to check any contract conditions imposed about future disclosures and examine those in conjunction with the exemptions from the Act.

The IC says in such a case where the deposit was subject to conditions: "it would be correct not to disclose information if there was a clear risk that the owner would demand return of the information or if the owner has a reasonable expectation that disclosure would amount to a breach of confidence. If in doubt the public authority which receives the request should check with the owner who will be able to advise the authority as to its wishes and expectations. In practice this means that where the owner of the information objects to its disclosure, an exemption can be found to cover this and prevent its release under FOI from occurring."

Exemptions which could apply are:

- Information available by other means;

- Personal Information;

- Information provided in confidence;

- Prejudice to commercial interests;

- Prejudice to effective conduct of public affairs.

If the information is due for future publication (even at an unspecified date), there would be a good public interest argument to withhold its disclosure until that time if the owner or indeed other depositors would be likely to withdraw the information.

Some private information is simply held on behalf of a third party, for example for preservation or security purposes. Perhaps the public authority may be holding the information as part of a service (whether for gain or otherwise) to the depositor. Although this information is in the possession of a public authority, it does not fall within the scope of the Act as the public authority has no interest in it. Although such information is not caught by the Act, the public authority would still have to respond to requests for it in some form.

This is because applicants can still make a request for this information and the public authority would still be under a duty to confirm or deny whether it holds the information. Although it would be under no obligation to supply the information, it would have to provide the applicant with advice and assistance to enable them to redirect their application to the person or body to which the information belongs. This would apply regardless of whether the other body is public authority or whether the applicant will in fact stand a chance of obtaining that information.

Environmental information

Environmental Information falls within a separate Access to Information regime, entitled the Environmental Information Regulations. The EIR relate to "information produced or received by that authority which is either in its possession or held by a person on its behalf". As such, all environmental information in the possession of a public authority would be covered by this legislation (subject to its exceptions), regardless of the reasons for its possession. However, the EIR contain an exception if disclosure would adversely affect the interests of the third party and the third party has not consented to disclosure.

Non-official information

Non-official information at the premises of a local authority would not be caught, provided that the information is not created by a member of staff in the course of their duties.

Examples of non-official information include:

Trade union communications

The trade union is a separate legal entity, and although it will represent the employees of a public authority, it does not have a role in respect of the functions of that public authority. The public authority has neither created this information nor does it retain the material for its own purposes. The public authority simply holds this information on behalf of, and as a service to, the trade union. As such, these communications would not be held for the purposes of Freedom of Information.

The IC says:

> "The only kind of trade union information that would be caught by the Act is that which is held by the public authority for the purposes of its official dealings with the trade union, and therefore held for the purposes of its functions as a public authority. Examples include minutes of joint meetings between management and the union and a public authority's trade union recognition agreement. Copies of such information in the possession of the trade union itself would not be subject to FOI, unless they were being held on behalf of the public authority."

Personal written communications (emails etc.)

Even if the private use of emails in the workplace were monitored, the public authority would still not 'hold' this information as it has no interest in it, unless disciplinary action were taken against a particular member(s) of staff. This is, however, an exception rather than the rule.

The IC says:

> "Problems may arise, however, in terms of hybrid emails, which contain a mixture of personal content and that relating to the duties of the employee. The information which falls within the latter classification is potentially disclosable, and so as part of good email management the formulation of such emails should be avoided."

Party political communications

A common example of party political communications would be emails between councillors which discuss party political matters. In this context the author will be communicating in their party political capacity and the emails would not relate to the functions of the public authority. These communications would therefore not be 'held' for the purposes of FOI.

(Further guidance on developing a policy for managing email is available from The National Archives: http://www.nationalarchives.gov.uk)

Codes of Practice

Sections 45 and 46 of the FOIA require the Secretary of State and Lord Chancellor to issue Codes of Practice which provide guidance to public authorities on 'desirable practice' in discharging their functions under Part I of the Act, and in relation to records management. These are very useful documents and are appended to this chapter. They were laid before Parliament as required by the Act on 20 November 2002. They do not have statutory force. However, failure to comply with the provisions of the Codes may lead to breach of the Act, and ultimately enforcement action being taken by the Information Commissioner.

The Code of Practice on the Discharge of Public Authorities' Functions under Part I of the Freedom of Information Act 2000 and Code of Practice on the Management of Records Under Section 46 of the Freedom of Information Act 2000, re the relevant codes.

Fees: charging for Freedom of Information

According to the Department for Constitutional Affairs (DCA), there is no charge for search and collation time for most requests under the Act. The rules say that public bodies can only refuse to answer a request on the grounds of cost if it would cost more than £450, which equates to about two and half days of searching time. For central government, the limit is £600, roughly three and a half days searching time.

In calculating costs, authorities can take into account the costs of determining whether the information is held, locating and retrieving it, and extracting the information (including editing). They cannot take into account the costs of considering whether information is exempt under the Act.

If a request would cost less than the appropriate limit, and there is no other basis on which it may be refused or otherwise dealt with, authorities must answer the request. The maximum fee that can be charged in these cases is limited to the specified costs of postage, printing and photocopying, but the DCA recommends that where the cost of communicating the information to the applicant is low, these charges should be waived.

The authority may charge a fee for requests that would cost more than the appropriate limit to answer, says the DCA, and where the costs would be particularly high the authorities should discuss with the applicant whether he would prefer to modify the request to reduce the cost. If the applicant does not agree with the proposed fee, he then has a right of appeal to the Information Commissioner.

The right to access information needs to be balanced by the need of public authorities to carry out their core duties. For this reason, the Act also allows for public authorities to refuse certain requests for information on the grounds of cost where these would be particularly expensive, even if the applicant is willing to pay for the information.

"This Government has maintained that there should be no financial barrier to people who want information about decisions taken about their children's schools, their hospitals, their police forces, and the other areas which affect their life," said Information Rights Minister Baroness Ashton. "The fees introduced today are designed to be easy for public bodies to operate, and to enable people to obtain most information for just the costs of printing, photocopying and postage."

Case Example

Case Ref: FS50075378
Date: 14/07/05
Public Authority: Ferryhill Town Council

Summary: The complainant requested information in relation to Council allotments and alleged that he was dissatisfied with the Fees Notice issued in response to his request. The Council stated that the cost of complying with the request would exceed the appropriate limit as identified in the Fees Regulations but they agreed to supply the information on receipt of the full costs. After approaching the Council for clarification the ICO was satisfied that they had estimated the costs in accordance with the Regulations. However, they did not give the complainant the opportunity to refine their request or offer to supply the information that could

be provided within the parameters of the appropriate limit. The Decision Notice therefore stipulated that the Council must offer appropriate advice and assistance to the complainant. **Section of Act/EIR & Finding: FOI s.9 – Not Upheld, FOI s.16 – Upheld.**

Fees can be charged for FOIA requests. The Freedom of Information and Data Protection (Appropriate Limit and Fees) Regulations 2004 SI 2004/3233 set out 'the appropriate amount' for the purposes of section 9A of the Data Protection Act 1998 and section 12 of the Freedom of Information Act 2000. If a public authority estimates that the cost of complying with a request for the information to which either of those provisions applies would exceed the appropriate amount, then the obligations which would otherwise be imposed by section 7 of the 1998 Act and section 1 of the 2000 Act, in respect of such requests for information, do not apply.

Regulation 3 prescribes an appropriate limit of £600 in the case of the public bodies listed in Part I of Schedule 1 to the 2000 Act (including government departments). An appropriate limit of £450 is prescribed in relation to all other public authorities.

Regulation 4 makes provision as to the costs to be estimated, and as to the manner in which they are to be estimated, for the purpose of estimating whether the cost of complying with a request would exceed the appropriate limit. The costs which may be taken into account are limited to those which the public authority reasonably expects to incur in undertaking certain specified activities in response to the request. Regulation 5 makes supplementary provision as to the estimation of costs in cases to which the 2000 Act applies. It provides that in relation to multiple requests which are related in specified ways by reference to those making the requests, the information to which the requests relate, and the timing of the requests, the estimated costs of complying with any single request is to be taken to be the aggregate estimated costs of complying with them all.

Regulation 6 makes provision as to the maximum fee that a public authority may specify in a fees notice under section 9 of the 2000 Act as a charge for complying with its duty under section 1(1) of the Act. The maximum is to be calculated by reference to specified limited aspects of the costs of informing the requester whether it holds the information and, if so, of communicating it to the requester.

Section 13 of the 2000 Act makes new provision for public authorities to be able to charge for the communication of information whose communication is not required because of the effect of the appropriate limit and is not otherwise required by law.

Regulation 7 makes provision as to the maximum fee that a public authority may charge for the communication of information in the exercise of that power. The maximum is to be calculated by reference to the total costs which may be taken into account in estimating whether the cost of complying with the request would exceed the appropriate limit (excluding any costs 'aggregated' from other requests), together with the full costs of informing the requester whether the information is held, and, if so, of communicating it to the requester.

Timing

The Freedom of Information (Time for Compliance with Request) Regulations 2004 (SI 2004/3364) deal with timing issues. Where a request is made under FOIA the applicant is entitled: (a) to be informed in writing by the public authority whether it holds information of the description specified in the request, and (b) if that is the case, to have that information communicated to him (section 1(1)).

Section 10(1) of the Act requires a public authority to comply with a request promptly, and in any event, not later than twenty working days following the date of receipt. Where the authority gives the applicant a fees notice, the working days in the period beginning with the day on which the fees notice is given to the applicant and ending with the day on which the fee is received by the authority are to be disregarded for the purpose of calculating the twentieth working day following the date of receipt referred to in section 10(1) (section 10(2)).

These Regulations are made under section 10(4) of the Act. They allow public authorities a longer maximum period of time than is provided under section 10(1) to comply with section 1(1) of the Act, provided that this longer period expires on a date not later than the sixtieth working day following the receipt of the request for information and subject to the obligation on the public authority to comply 'promptly'.

Regulation 3 provides that where a request for information is received by the governing body of a maintained school or maintained nursery school, or relates to information that is situated in a school maintained by the Secretary of State for Defence, for the purposes of section 10(1) or (2) working days which are not school days are not to be taken into account in calculating the twentieth working

day following the date of receipt. The public authority must comply with the request within twenty working days of the date of receipt, disregarding any working day which, in relation to the school, is not a school day, or within sixty working days following the date of receipt, whichever is the sooner.

The explanatory note says:

> "The governing body of a maintained school or maintained nursery school is a public authority, as defined in section 3 of the Act. A body can be a public authority either by:
>
> 1.   being listed in Schedule 1 to the Act;
>
> 2.   being designated by order under section 5 of the Act; or
>
> 3.   being a publicly-owned company as defined by section 6 of the Act.
>
> The governing body of a maintained school or maintained nursery school is listed at paragraph 52 in Part IV of Schedule 1 to the Act, as substituted by section 215 of, and paragraph 127 of Schedule 21 to, the Education Act 2002."

Regulation 4 allows appropriate records authorities and places of deposit appointed under section 4(1) of the Public Records Act 1958 up to thirty working days from the date of receipt to comply with a request for information, where the information requested relates to information held in a transferred public record that has not been designated as open information for the purposes of section 66 of the Act. 'Transferred public record' is defined in section 15(4) of the Act, and means a public record which has been transferred to either the National Archives (formerly the Public Record Office), a place of deposit appointed by the Lord Chancellor under the Public Records Act 1958 ('the 1958 Act'), or to the Public Record Office of Northern Ireland. 'Appropriate records authority' is defined in section 15(5) of the Act and, in relation to a transferred public record, means:

- the National Archives, in relation to a record transferred to the National Archives;

- the Lord Chancellor, in relation to a record transferred to a place of deposit appointed by the Lord Chancellor under the 1958 Act; and

- the Public Record Office of Northern Ireland, in relation to a record transferred to that Office.

Regulation 5 provides that the Information Commissioner may exercise his discretion where a public authority cannot comply with the request within the time period referred to in section 10(1) or (2) because the information to which it relates

needs to be obtained from an individual who is actively involved in an operation of the armed forces of the Crown, or in the preparations for such an operation, and allow the public authority to comply with the request by some later specified date, not being later than the sixtieth working day following the receipt of the request.

Regulation 6 provides that the Information Commissioner may exercise his discretion where a public authority cannot comply with the request within the time period referred to in section 10(1) or (2) because the information to which it relates may not be present in the United Kingdom or may require information not present in the United Kingdom in order to comply with it, and allow the public authority to comply with the request by some later specified date, not being later than the sixtieth working day following the receipt of the request.

Under both Regulations 5 and 6, the public authority must apply to the Information Commissioner to exercise this discretion within twenty working days following the date of receipt of the request.

Statutory prohibitions on disclosure

The Freedom of Information (Removal and Relaxation of Statutory Prohibitions on Disclosure of Information) Order 2004 (SI 2004/3363) deal with some disclosure issues.

Section 75 of the FOIA gives the Secretary of State the power to make an order to repeal or amend an enactment for the purpose of removing or relaxing a prohibition that, by virtue of section 44(1)(a) of the Act, is capable of preventing disclosure under section 1 of the Act.

Section 1 of these regulations gives any person who makes a request to a public authority for information the right to:

a) be informed in writing whether the public authority holds the information of the description specified in the request; and

b) if that is the case, to have that information communicated to him.

Section 44(1)(a) provides that information is exempt from disclosure under section 1 if its disclosure, otherwise than under the Act, by the public authority holding it is prohibited by or under any enactment.

The changes in the regulations are appended to this chapter.

On 16th June 2005 the Department for Constitutional Affairs said it was looking further at whether other regulations were needed. It issued a *'Report on the government's review of statutory prohibitions on disclosure'*. This report sets out all the enactments which have been reviewed and indicates whether the government intends to repeal or amend them using powers in the Freedom of Information Act 2000.

Information about employees

The IC 's office has issued guidance for public bodies about issuing information about their employees. Caution must be exercised. An irate parent whose children have rightly been taken into care may want to take personal physical vengeance on the official responsible. The local authority should not blithely give such information out nor could it under the Data Protection 1998 either.

The guidance suggests the following practical suggestions:

- Draw a distinction between professional information – e.g. job titles or sectoral responsibilities, and genuinely personal or sensitive information such as reasons for sickness absence. Build this into a disclosure policy and make staff aware of it.

- Audit the information kept about employees. Can any reassurances be given to them that certain information will never be disclosed in response to an access request? Is there any information that will always be provided on request or included in a publication scheme? This needs to be explained to staff.

- Consider any differences in the degree of access that should be given to information about senior/junior staff, or ones in particular roles. Public authorities should consider linking their policy for the disclosure of information to staff seniority or function and should communicate this to their employees.

- Inform staff of the policy for disclosing information about them. Information should be put in staff handbooks and any necessary training should be carried out. The rules relating to disclosure should be made clear to individuals commencing employment with the public authority.

- When a request for disclosure is received, tell any staff members affected about it and take any objections into account. Remember that public authorities may have to deal with cases where information is disclosed

despite an employee's objection to this, be prepared to deal with such situations.

- Public authorities should include in their publication scheme any information about their employees that they would disclose as a matter of routine.

Further information

The Legislation and Statutory Codes of Practice: the following legislation is available on the IC's web site:

Freedom of Information Act 2000:

Statutory Instrument on fees – The Freedom of Information and Data Protection (Appropriate Limit and Fees) Regulations 2004 SI 2004/ 3233 can be found at http://www.opsi.gov.uk/si/si2004/20043244.htm

Statutory Instrument to time for compliance:

The Freedom of Information (Time for Compliance with Request) Regulations 2004 (SI 2004/3364) can be found at: http://www.opsi.gov.uk/si/si2004/20043364.htm

Statutory Instrument on the relaxation of statutory bars:

The Freedom of Information (Removal and Relaxation of Statutory Prohibitions on Disclosure of Information) Order 2004 (SI 2004/3363) can be found at http://www.opsi.gov.uk/si/si2004/20043363.htm

For the June 2005 Review of this area see – http://www.dca.gov.uk/Statutory-BarsReport2005.pdf

S45 Code of Practice – appended to this chapter

S46 Code of Practice – appended to this chapter

For a full list of the secondary instruments made under the Act please visit the DCA's website at http://www.dca.gov.uk/majrepfr.htm#statdisc

Scottish public authorities

The Act applies to public authorities in England, Wales and Northern Ireland. Access to information held by Scottish public authorities is provided by the Freedom of Information (Scotland) Act 2002 and the Scottish Environmental

Information Regulations. For more information see the Scottish Information Commissioner's website at http://www.itspublicknowledge.info/

Procedural Guidance

The following procedural guidance is available from the IC's office and on their web site:

Advice and Assistance	Awareness Guidance 23
Records Managements FAQs	Awareness Guidance 8
Time for Compliance	Awareness Guidance 11
Vexatious and Repeated Requests	Awareness Guidance 22
When is Information caught by the Freedom of Information Act? (Summarised in this chapter 2)	Awareness Guidance 12

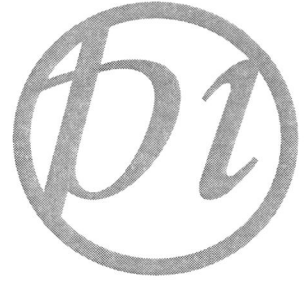

Appendices to Chapter 2

Appendices to Chapter 2

Appendix 1: Provisions in the Freedom of Information (Removal and Relaxation of Statutory Prohibitions on Disclosure of Information) Order 2004 (SI 2004/3363)

Article 2 to the Order inserts a new section 154A into the Factories Act 1961. Section 154 makes it an offence for a person to disclose information about any manufacturing process or trade secret that he has obtained in pursuance of powers conferred by sections 148 or 153 of the Factories Act 1961, unless that disclosure is made in the performance of his duty. By section 154A, the offence provisions in section 154 do not apply if the person making the disclosure is, or is acting on behalf of a person who is, a public authority for the purposes of the Act.

Article 3 inserts a new section 59A into the Offices, Shops and Railway Premises Act 1963 ("the 1963 Act"). Section 59 of the 1963 Act makes it an offence for a person to disclose information he has obtained from premises that he has entered in the exercise of powers conferred by the 1963 Act, unless that disclosure is made in the performance of his duty or for the purposes of any legal proceedings, or of a report of any such proceedings. By section 59A, the offence provision in section 59 does not apply if the person making the disclosure is, or is acting on behalf of a person who is, a public authority for the purposes of the Act.

Article 4 inserts a new subsection (1A) after subsection (1) of section 118 of the Medicines Act 1968 ('the 1968 Act'). Section 118 of the 1968 Act provides that where a person discloses to any other person certain information he shall be guilty of an offence, unless the disclosure was made in the performance of his duty. Section 118 relates to information about any manufacturing process or trade secret obtained by entry to premises by virtue of section 111 of the 1968 Act, or to any information obtained by or furnished to that person in pursuance of the 1968 Act. By section 118(1A), the offence provision in section 118(1) does not apply if the person making the disclosure is, or is acting on behalf of a person who is, a public authority for the purposes of the Act.

Article 5 amends section 28 of the Health and Safety At Work etc Act 1974 ('the 1974 Act'). Section 28(2) of the 1974 Act contains a general prohibition on the disclosure of 'relevant information', which is defined by section 28(1)(a) as being information that is obtained by a person under section 27(1) of the 1974 Act, or furnished to any person under section 27A by virtue of section 43A(6) of the 1974 Act or in pursuance of a requirement imposed by any of the relevant statutory provisions. The 'relevant statutory provisions' are specified in section 53 of the 1974 Act. Article 5(2) inserts a new subparagraph (f) after subsection (3)(e) in section 28, creating a further gateway for the disclosure of relevant information by a recipient where the recipient is, or is acting on behalf of a person who is, a public authority for the purposes of the Act. A 'recipient', in relation to any relevant information, means the person by whom the information was obtained or to whom it was furnished (section 28(1)(b) of the 1974 Act).

Article 5(3) amends section 28(5) of the 1974 Act so that a person to whom information is disclosed pursuant to the new section 28(3)(f) is not prohibited from further disclosing that information.

Article 5(4) inserts a new subsection (9A) after subsection (9) of section 28 of the 1974 Act, which disapplies the provisions of subsection (7) of section 28 where the person who has obtained information in the exercise of powers under sections 14(4)(a) and 20 of the 1974 Act is, or is acting on behalf of a person who is, a public authority for the purposes of the Act. Subsection (7) of section 28 prohibits the disclosure of information obtained in the exercise of those powers, except for the purposes of: the discloser's functions; any legal proceedings or any investigation or inquiry held by virtue of section 14(2) of the 1974 Act or for the purposes of a report of any such proceedings or inquiry, or of a special report made by virtue of that section; or with consent.

Article 6 repeals section 5 of the Biological Standards Act 1975. Section 5 provides that a person is guilty of an offence if he discloses any information obtained by him in the course of and by virtue of his membership of or employment by the National Biological Standards Board and which relates to a manufacturing process or a trade secret, unless the disclosure is made in the performance of his office or employment.

Article 7 inserts a new paragraph 5A after paragraph 5 of Schedule 11 to the National Health Service Act 1977 ('the 1977 Act'). Paragraph 5 of Schedule 11 to the 1977 Act prohibits any person who obtains information under section 57 of that Act, otherwise than in connection with the execution of that section and Schedule 11, or of an order made under that section, from disclosing information unless that disclosure is for the purposes of criminal proceedings, or of a

report of any criminal proceedings, or with permission granted by or on behalf of a Minister of the Crown. By the new paragraph 5A, the restrictions in paragraph 5 do not apply if the person who has obtained any information as is referred to in that paragraph is, or is acting on behalf of a person who is, a public authority for the purposes of the Act.

Article 8 amends section 49 of the Audit Commission Act 1998 ('the 1998 Act'). Article 8(2) removes the restrictions on the disclosure of information obtained in the course of any study pursuant to any provision of the 1998 Act or of Part I of the Local Government Act 1999. Article 8(3) creates a new section 49A which relates to disclosure of information obtained under the 1998 Act or Part 1 of the Local Government Act 1999 by a person who is, or is acting on behalf of a person who is, a public authority for the purposes of the Act. Such information may be disclosed in any circumstances, including those in which disclosure would be authorised (but for section 49(1A)) under section 49(1), except where disclosure would, or would be likely to, prejudice the performance by such a person of any of his statutory functions. A person to whom section 49A(2) applies who discloses information otherwise than as authorised by subsection (2) is guilty of an offence and liable on summary conviction to a fine not exceeding the statutory maximum.

Article 9 amends section 20 of the Access to Justice Act 1999, by inserting new subsections (4A) and (4B) after subsection (4) of that section. These provide, in relation to the disclosure of information by a person who is, or is acting on behalf of a person who is, a public authority for the purposes of the Freedom of Information Act 2000, once the period of one hundred years starting at the end of the calendar year in which a record containing the information was created has expired, nothing in section 20(1) of the Access to Justice Act 1999 shall prohibit the disclosure of information.

Appendix 2: The s45 Code of Practice

Secretary of State for Constitutional Affairs' Code of Practice on the discharge of public authorities' functions under Part I of the Freedom of Information Act 2000. Issued under section 45 of the Act. November 2004

Presented to Parliament by the Secretary of State for Constitutional Affairs pursuant to section 45(5) of the Freedom of Information Act 2000.

FOREWORD

- Introduction

- Role of the Information Commissioner

- Part I of the Freedom of Information Act

- Procedures and Training

- Further Guidance

CODE OF PRACTICE

- I Introduction

- II The provision of advice and assistance to persons making requests for information

- III Transferring requests for information

- IV Consultation with Third Parties

- V Freedom of Information and confidentiality obligations

- VI Complaints procedures

Foreword

INTRODUCTION

1. The Code of Practice, to which this is a foreword, fulfils the duty of the Secretary of State set out in section 45 of the Freedom of Information Act 2000, to provide guidance to public authorities as to the practice which it would, in his opinion, be desirable for them to follow in connection with the discharge of their functions under Part I of the Act. It is envisaged that Regulations to be made with respect to environmental information will make provision for the issue by the

Secretary of State of a Code of Practice applying to the discharge of authorities' functions under those Regulations.

2. This foreword does not form part of the Code itself.

3. The Government is committed to greater openness in the public sector. The Freedom of Information Act will further this aim by helping to transform the culture of the public sector to one of greater openness, enabling members of the public to better understand the decisions of public authorities, and ensuring that services provided by the public sector are seen to be efficiently and properly delivered. Conformity with the Code will assist this.

4. The aims of the Code are to:

   • facilitate the disclosure of information under the Act by setting out good administrative practice that it is desirable for public authorities to follow when handling requests for information, including, where appropriate, the transfer of a request to a different authority;

   • protect the interests of applicants by setting out standards for the provision of advice which it would be good practice to make available to them and to encourage the development of effective means of complaining about decisions taken under the Act;

   • facilitate consideration by public authorities of the interests of third parties who may be affected by any decision to disclose information, by setting standards for consultation; and

   • promote consideration by public authorities of the implications for Freedom of Information before agreeing to confidentiality provisions in contracts and accepting information in confidence from a third party more generally.

ROLE OF THE INFORMATION COMMISSIONER

5. The Information Commissioner has a duty under section 47 of the Act to promote the following of good practice by public authorities, and in particular to promote observance of the requirements of the Act and of the provisions of this Code of Practice. The Act confers a number of powers on him to enable him to carry out that duty specifically in relation to the Code.

PRACTICE RECOMMENDATIONS

6. If it appears to the Commissioner that the practice of a public authority in relation to the exercise of its functions under the Act does not conform with that proposed in this Code of Practice, he may give to the authority a recommendation, under section 48 (known as a 'practice recommendation'), specifying the steps which should, in his opinion, be taken for promoting such conformity.

7. A practice recommendation must be given in writing and must refer to the particular provisions of the Code of Practice with which, in the Commissioner's opinion, the public authority's practice does not conform. A practice recommendation is simply a recommendation and cannot be directly enforced by the Information Commissioner. However, a failure to comply with a practice recommendation may lead to a failure to comply with the Act. Further, a failure to take account of a practice recommendation may lead to an adverse comment in a report to Parliament by the Commissioner.

8. It should be noted that because the provisions of the Act relating to the general right of access will not be brought into force until 1 January 2005, the Commissioner's powers to issue practice recommendations in relation to the handling of individual requests for information under the general rights of access will not take effect before that date.

DECISION AND ENFORCEMENT NOTICES

9. The Commissioner may also refer to non-compliance with the Code in decision notices issued as a result of a complaint under s.50 of the Act and enforcement notices issued under s.52 of the Act where, irrespective of any complaints that may have been received, the Commissioner considers that a public authority has failed to comply with any requirement of Part 1 of the Act. Where relevant, the Commissioner will make reference to the specific provisions of the Code in specifying the steps to be taken to ensure compliance with the Act.

INFORMATION NOTICES

10. If the Information Commissioner reasonably requires any information for the purpose of determining whether the practice of a public authority conforms to the Code, under section 51 of the Act he may serve an 'information notice' on the authority, requiring it to provide specified information relating to its conformity with the Code.

COMPLIANCE WITH NOTICES

11. Under the provisions of section 54 of the Act, if a public authority fails to comply with a decisions, information or enforcement notice, the Commissioner may certify in writing to the court that the public authority has failed to comply with that notice. The court may then inquire into the matter and, after hearing any witnesses who may be produced against or on behalf of, the public authority, and after hearing any statement that may be offered in defence, deal with the authority as if it had committed a contempt of court.

PART I OF THE FREEDOM OF INFORMATION ACT

12. The Code provides guidance on good practice for public authorities in connection with the discharge of their functions under Part I of the Act. The main features of Part I Freedom of Information Act 2000 are:

    - general rights of access in relation to recorded information held by public authorities, subject to certain conditions and exemptions;

    - in cases where access to information is refused in reliance on an exemption from disclosure, a duty on public authorities to give reasons for that refusal;

    - a duty to provide reasonable advice and assistance to applicants approaching public authorities seeking information;

    - a duty on every public authority to adopt and maintain a publication scheme, approved by the Commissioner, which relates to the publication of information by the authority, and to publish information in accordance with the scheme (an authority may adopt a model publication scheme approved by the Commissioner).

DUTY TO PROVIDE ADVICE AND ASSISTANCE

13. Section 16 of the Act places a duty on public authorities to provide reasonable advice and assistance to applicants. A public authority is to be taken to have complied with this duty in any particular case if it has conformed with the provisions of this Code in relation to the provision of advice and assistance in that case. The duty to assist and advise is enforceable by the Information Commissioner. If a public authority fails in its statutory duty, the Commissioner may issue a decision notice under section 50, or an enforcement notice under section 52.

14. Public authorities should not forget that other Acts of Parliament may be relevant to the way in which authorities provide advice and assistance to applicants or potential applicants, e.g. the Disability Discrimination Act 1995 and the Race Relations Act 1976 (as amended by the Race Relations (Amendment) Act 2000).

PROCEDURES AND TRAINING

15. All communications in writing to a public authority, including those transmitted by electronic means, may contain or amount to requests for information within the meaning of the Act, and so must be dealt with in accordance with the provisions of the Act. While in many cases such requests will be dealt with in the course of normal business, it is essential that public authorities dealing with correspondence, or which otherwise may be required to provide information, have in place procedures for taking decisions at appropriate levels, and ensure that sufficient staff are familiar with the requirements of the Act and the Codes of Practice issued under its provisions. Staff dealing with correspondence should also take account of any relevant guidance on good practice issued by the Commissioner. Authorities should ensure that proper training is provided in this regard. Larger authorities should ensure that they have a central core of staff with particular expertise in Freedom of Information who can provide expert advice to other members of staff as needed.

16. In planning and delivering training authorities should be aware of other provisions affecting the disclosure of information such as Environmental Information Regulations and the Data Protection Act 1998.

FURTHER GUIDANCE

17. The DCA has produced a suite of guidance which provides advice for public authorities in order to help them fulfil their obligations under the Freedom of Information Act. Of particular relevance to authorities will be the Guidance on Processing Requests, which provides detailed advice on handling requests for information. The suite of guidance also includes detailed guidance on the application of exemptions. This should be referred to for further guidance on the factors which should be taken into account when considering whether exemptions apply.

18. The Information Commissioner's Office have also issued 'Awareness Guides' on its web-site. Again, these Awareness Guides provide detailed, practical guidance on best practice which should be followed by public authorities. The Commissioner will also publish the internal

advice developed for use by complaint caseworkers and summaries of complaint cases considered by the Commissioner and the Tribunal.

19. More specialist advice on the Act is also available from representative bodies (for instance the Local Government Association and the Association of Chief Police Officers) and by Government Departments for small public authorities falling within their general policy areas (for instance the DfES for schools).

CODE OF PRACTICE

(Freedom of Information Act 2000, section 45)

Guidance to public authorities as to the practice which it would be desirable for them to follow in connection with the discharge of their functions under Part I of the Freedom of Information Act 2000

Having consulted the Information Commissioner, this Code of Practice is issued by the Secretary of State for Constitutional Affairs under section 45 of the Freedom of Information Act 2000 (c.36) on 25 November 2004. The Code provides guidance to public authorities, as defined in the Act, as to the practice which it would, in the Secretary of State's opinion, be desirable for them to follow in connection with the discharge of their functions under Part I of the Act.

Laid before Parliament on 25 November 2004 pursuant to section 45(5) of the Freedom of Information Act 2000.

I Introduction

1. This Code of Practice provides guidance to public authorities as to the practice which it would, in the opinion of the Secretary of State for Constitutional Affairs, be desirable for them to follow in connection with the discharge of their functions under Part I (Access to information held by public authorities) of the Freedom of Information Act 2000 ('the Act').

2. Words and expressions used in this Code have the same meaning as the same words and expressions used in the Act.

II The provision of advice and assistance to persons making requests for information

3. The following paragraphs of this Code apply in relation to the provision of advice and assistance to persons who propose to make, or have made, requests for information to public authorities. They are intended to provide guidance to public authorities as to the practice which it would be desirable for them to follow in the discharge of their duty under section 16 of the Act.

ADVICE AND ASSISTANCE TO THOSE PROPOSING TO MAKE REQUESTS

4. Public authorities should publish their procedures for dealing with requests for information. Consideration should be given to including in these procedures a statement of:

   • what the public authority's usual procedure will be where it does not hold the information requested (see also III – 'Transferring requests for information'), and

   • when the public authority may need to consult other public authorities and/or third parties in order to reach a decision on whether the requested information can be released (see also IV – 'Consultation with third parties'),

5. The procedures should include an address or addresses (including an e-mail address where possible) to which applicants may direct requests for information or for assistance. A telephone number should also be provided, where possible that of a named individual who can provide assistance. These procedures should be referred to in the authority's publication scheme.

6. Staff working in public authorities in contact with the public should bear in mind that not everyone will be aware of the Act, or Regulations made under it, and they will need where appropriate to draw these to the attention of potential applicants who appear unaware of them.

7. Where a person is unable to frame his or her request in writing, the public authority should ensure that appropriate assistance is given to enable that person to make a request for information. Depending on the circumstances, consideration should be given to:

   • advising the person that another person or agency (such as a Citizens Advice Bureau) may be able to assist them with the application, or make the application on their behalf;

- in exceptional circumstances, offering to take a note of the application over the telephone and then send the note to the applicant for confirmation (in which case the written note of the telephone request, once verified by the applicant and returned, would constitute a written request for information and the statutory time limit for reply would begin when the written confirmation was received).

This list is not exhaustive, and public authorities should be flexible in offering advice and assistance most appropriate to the circumstances of the applicant.

CLARIFYING THE REQUEST

8. A request for information must adequately specify and describe the information sought by the applicant. Public authorities are entitled to ask for more detail, if needed, to enable them to identify and locate the information sought. Authorities should, as far as reasonably practicable, provide assistance to the applicant to enable him or her to describe more clearly the information requested.

9. Authorities should be aware that the aim of providing assistance is to clarify the nature of the information sought, not to determine the aims or motivation of the applicant. Care should be taken not to give the applicant the impression that he or she is obliged to disclose the nature of his or her interest as a precondition to exercising the rights of access, or that he or she will be treated differently if he or she does (or does not). Public authorities should be prepared to explain to the applicant why they are asking for more information. It is important that the applicant is contacted as soon as possible, preferably by telephone, fax or e-mail, where more information is needed to clarify what is sought.

10. Appropriate assistance in this instance might include:

    - providing an outline of the different kinds of information which might meet the terms of the request;

    - providing access to detailed catalogues and indexes, where these are available, to help the applicant ascertain the nature and extent of the information held by the authority;

    - providing a general response to the request setting out options for further information which could be provided on request.

This list is not exhaustive, and public authorities should be flexible in offering advice and assistance most appropriate to the circumstances of the applicant.

11. In seeking to clarify what is sought, public authorities should bear in mind that applicants cannot reasonably be expected to possess identifiers such as a file reference number, or a description of a particular record, unless this information is made available by the authority for the use of applicants.

LIMITS TO ADVICE AND ASSISTANCE

12. If, following the provision of such assistance, the applicant still fails to describe the information requested in a way which would enable the authority to identify and locate it, the authority is not expected to seek further clarification. The authority should disclose any information relating to the application which has been successfully identified and found for which it does not propose to claim an exemption. It should also explain to the applicant why it cannot take the request any further and provide details of the authority's complaints procedure and the applicant's rights under section 50 of the Act (see 'Complaints Procedure' in section VI).

ADVICE AND ASSISTANCE AND FEES

13. Where the applicant indicates that he or she is not prepared to pay the fee notified in any fees notice given to the applicant, the authority should consider whether there is any information that may be of interest to the applicant that is available free of charge.

14. Where an authority is not obliged to comply with a request for information because, under section 12(1) and regulations made under section 12, the cost of complying would exceed the 'appropriate limit' (i.e. cost threshold) the authority should consider providing an indication of what, if any, information could be provided within the cost ceiling. The authority should also consider advising the applicant that by reforming or re-focussing their request, information may be able to be supplied for a lower, or no, fee.

15. An authority is not expected to provide assistance to applicants whose requests are vexatious within the meaning of section 14 of the Act. Guidance on what constitutes a vexatious request can be found in the DCA Handbook – 'Guidance on Processing Requests'. The Information Commissioner has also issued advice on dealing with vexatious and repetitious requests.

III Transferring requests for information

16. The following paragraphs apply in any case in which a public authority is not able to comply with a request (or to comply with it in full) because it does not hold the information requested, and proposes, in accordance with section 1(1)(a), to confirm that it does not hold that information.

17. If the authority has reason to believe that some or all of the information requested, but which it does not hold, is held by another public authority, the authority should consider what would be the most helpful way of assisting the applicant with his or her request.

18. In most cases this is likely to involve:

    • contacting the applicant and informing him or her that the information requested may be held by another public authority;

    • suggesting that the applicant re-applies to the authority which the original authority believes may hold the information; and

    • providing him or her with contact details for that authority.

19. However, in some cases the authority to which the original request is made may consider it to be more appropriate to transfer the request to another authority in respect of the information which it does not hold. In such cases, the authority should consult the other authority with a view to ascertaining whether it does in fact hold the information and, if so, whether it is obliged to confirm this under section 1(1) of the Act. If that is the case, the first authority should proceed to consider transferring the request. A request (or part of a request) should not be transferred without confirmation by the second authority that it holds the information, and will confirm as much to the applicant on receipt of a request.

20. Before transferring a request for information to another authority, the original authority should consider:

    • whether a transfer is appropriate; and if so

    • whether the applicant is likely to have any grounds to object to the transfer. If the authority reasonably concludes that the applicant is not likely to object, it may transfer the request without going back to the applicant, but should tell him or her it has done so.

21. Where there are reasonable grounds to believe an applicant is likely to object, the authority should only transfer the request to another

authority with his or her consent. If the authority is in any doubt, it may prefer to advise the applicant to make a new request to the other authority, and to inform the applicant that the other authority has confirmed that it holds the information.

22. Where a request or part of a request is transferred from one public authority to another, the receiving authority should comply with its obligations under Part I of the Act in the same way as it would in the case of a request that is received direct from an applicant. The time for complying with such a request should be calculated by regarding the date of transfer as the date of receipt of the request.

23. All transfers of requests should take place as soon as is practicable, and the applicant must be informed as soon as possible once this has been done.

24. Where a public authority is unable either to advise the applicant which public authority holds, or may hold, the requested information or to facilitate the transfer of the request to another authority (or considers it inappropriate to do so) it should consider what advice, if any, it can provide to the applicant to enable him or her to pursue his or her request.

IV Consultation with Third Parties

25. There are many circumstances in which:

- requests for information may relate to persons other than the applicant and the authority; or

- disclosure of information is likely to affect the interests of persons other than the applicant or the authority.

26. It is highly recommended that public authorities take appropriate steps to ensure that such third parties, and those who supply public authorities with information, are aware of the public authority's duty to comply with the Freedom of Information Act, and that therefore information will have to be disclosed upon request unless an exemption applies.

27. In some cases is will be necessary to consult, directly and individually, with such persons in order to determine whether or not an exemption applies to the information requested, or in order to reach a view on whether the obligations in section 1 of the Act arise in relation to that information. But in a range of other circumstances it will be good

practice to do so; for example where a public authority proposes to disclose information relating to third parties, or information which is likely to affect their interests, reasonable steps should, where appropriate, be taken to give them advance notice, or failing that, to draw it to their attention afterwards.

28.   In some cases, it may also be appropriate to consult such third parties about such matters as whether any further explanatory material or advice should be given to the applicant together with the information in question. Such advice may, for example, refer to any restrictions (including copyright restrictions) which may exist as to the subsequent use which may be made of such information.

29.   No decision to release information which has been supplied by one government department to another should be taken without first notifying, and where appropriate consulting, the department from which the information originated.

30.   Where information to be disclosed relates to a number of third parties, or the interests of a number of third parties may be affected by a disclosure, and those parties have a representative organisation which can express views on behalf of those parties, the authority may consider whether it would be sufficient to notify or consult with that representative organisation. If there is no representative organisation, the authority may consider that it would be sufficient to notify or consult with a representative sample of the third parties in question.

V Freedom of Information and confidentiality obligations

31.   Public authorities should bear clearly in mind their obligations under the Freedom of Information Act when preparing to enter into contracts which may contain terms relating to the disclosure of information by them.

32.   When entering into contracts with non-public authority contractors, public authorities may be asked to accept confidentiality clauses, for example to the effect that information relating to the terms of the contract, its value and performance will not be disclosed. Public authorities should carefully consider the compatibility of such terms with their obligations under the Act. It is important that both the public authority and the contractor are aware of the limits placed by the Act on the enforceability of such confidentiality clauses.

33. The Act does, however, recognise that there will be circumstances and respects in which the preservation of confidentiality between public authority and contractor is appropriate, and must be maintained, in the public interest.

34. Where there is good reason, as recognised by the terms of the exemption provisions of the Act, to include non-disclosure provisions in a contract, public authorities should consider the desirability where possible of making express provision in the contract identifying the information which should not be disclosed and the reasons for confidentiality. Consideration may also be given to including provision in contracts as to when consultation with third parties will be necessary or appropriate before the information is disclosed.

35. Similar considerations will apply to the offering or acceptance of confidentiality obligations by public authorities in non-contractual circumstances. There will be circumstances in which such obligations will be an appropriate part of the acquisition of information from third parties and will be protected by the terms of the exemption provisions of the Act. But again, it will be important that both the public authority and the third party are aware of the limits placed by the Act on the enforceability of expectations of confidentiality, and for authorities to ensure that such expectations are created only where to do so is consistent with their obligations under the Act.

VI Complaints procedure

36. Each public authority should have a procedure in place for dealing with complaints both in relation to its handling of requests for information. The same procedure could also usefully handle complaints in relation to the authority's publication scheme. If the complaints cannot be dealt with swiftly and satisfactorily on an informal basis, the public authority should inform persons if approached by them of the details of its internal complaints procedure, and how to contact the Information Commissioner, if the complainant wishes to write to him about the matter.

37. When communicating any decision made to refusing a request, in reliance on an exemption provision, public authorities are obliged, under section 17(7) of the Act notify the applicant of particulars of the procedure provided by the public authority for dealing with complaints (or to state that it does not have one). In doing so, they should provide full details of their own complaints procedure, including how to make

a complaint and inform the applicant of the right to complain to the Commissioner under section 50 if he or she is still dissatisfied following the authority's review.

38. Any written reply from the applicant (including one transmitted by electronic means) expressing dissatisfaction with an authority's response to a request for information should be treated as a complaint, as should any written communication from a person who considers that the authority is not complying with its publication scheme. These communications should be handled in accordance with the authority's complaints procedure, even if, in the case of a request for information under the general rights of access, the applicant does not expressly state his or her desire for the authority to review its decision or its handling of the application.

39. The complaints procedure should provide a fair and thorough review of handling issues and of decisions taken pursuant to the Act, including decisions taken about where the public interest lies in respect of exempt information. It should enable a fresh decision to be taken on a reconsideration of all the factors relevant to the issue. Complaints procedures should be as clear and simple as possible. They should encourage a prompt determination of the complaint.

40. Where the complaint concerns a request for information under the general rights of access, the review should be undertaken by someone senior to the person who took the original decision, where this is reasonably practicable. The public authority should in any event undertake a full re-evaluation of the case, taking into account the matters raised by the investigation of the complaint.

41. In all cases, complaints should be acknowledged promptly and the complainant should be informed of the authority's target date for determining the complaint. Where it is apparent that determination of the complaint will take longer than the target time (for example because of the complexity of the particular case), the authority should inform the applicant and explain the reason for the delay. The complainant should always be informed of the outcome of his or her complaint.

42. Authorities should set their own target times for dealing with complaints; these should be reasonable, and subject to regular review. Each public authority should publish its target times for determining complaints and information as to how successful it is with meeting those targets.

43. Records should be kept of all complaints and of their outcome. Authorities should have procedures in place for monitoring complaints and for reviewing, and, if necessary, amending, procedures for dealing with requests for information where such action is indicated by more than occasional reversals of initial decisions.

44. Where the outcome of a complaint is a decision that information should be disclosed which was previously withheld, the information in question should be disclosed as soon as practicable and the applicant should be informed how soon this will be.

45. Where the outcome of a complaint is that the procedures within an authority have not been properly followed by the authority's staff, the authority should apologise to the applicant. The authority should also take appropriate steps to prevent similar errors occurring in future.

46. Where the outcome of a complaint is that an initial decision to withhold information is upheld, or is otherwise in the authority's favour, the applicant should be informed of his or her right to apply to the Commissioner, and be given details of how to make an application, for a decision on whether the request for information has been dealt with in accordance with the requirements of Part I of the Act.

Appendix 3: S46 Code of Practice

Lord Chancellor's Code of Practice on the Management of Records. Issued under section 46 of the Freedom of Information Act 2000. November 2002

FOREWORD

- General

- Authorities subject to the Public Records Acts

THE CODE OF PRACTICE

- Introduction

PART I: RECORDS MANAGEMENT

- Functional responsibility

- Policy

- Human resources

- Active records management

- Disposal arrangements

- Management of electronic records

PART II

- Review and Transfer of Public Records

ANNEX A

- Standards accepted in Records Management

Foreword

GENERAL

1.   This Code of Practice (hereafter referred to as 'the Code') provides guidance to all public authorities as to the practice which it would, in the opinion of the Lord Chancellor, be desirable for them to follow in connection with the discharge of their functions under the Freedom of Information Act 2000 (FOIA). The Code applies also to other bodies

that are subject to the Public Records Act 1958 and the Public Records Act (NI) 1923.

2.   The Code fulfils the duty of the Lord Chancellor under section 46 of the FOIA.

3.   Any freedom of information legislation is only as good as the quality of the records to which it provides access. Such rights are of little use if reliable records are not created in the first place, if they cannot be found when needed or if the arrangements for their eventual archiving or destruction are inadequate. Consequently, all public authorities are strongly encouraged to pay heed to the guidance in the Code.

4.   The Code is a supplement to the provisions in the FOIA. But its adoption will help authorities to comply with their duties under that Act. It is not a substitute for legislation. Public authorities should seek legal advice as appropriate on general issues relating to the implementation of the FOIA, or its application to individual cases. The Code is complemented by the Code of Practice under section 45 of the FOIA and by Memoranda of Understanding setting out how the consultation requirements of section 66 of the FOIA will be put into effect.

5.   The Information Commissioner will promote the observance of the Code by public authorities, acting as required by the FOIA. If it appears to the Commissioner that the practice of an authority in relation to the exercise of its functions under the FOIA does not conform with that set out in the Code, he may issue a practice recommendation under section 48 of the Act. A practice recommendation must be in writing and must specify the provisions of the Code which have not been met and the steps which should, in his opinion, be taken to promote conformity with Code.

6.   If the Commissioner reasonably requires any information for the purpose of determining whether the practice of a public authority in relation to the exercise of its functions under the FOIA conforms with that proposed in this Code, he may serve on the authority a notice (known as an 'information notice') under the provisions of section 51 of the Act. This requires it, within such time as is specified in the notice, to furnish the Commissioner, in such form as may be so specified, with such information relating to conformity with the Code of Practice as is so specified.

7.   An information notice must contain a statement that the Commissioner regards the specified information as relevant for the purpose of deciding

whether the practice of the authority conforms with that proposed in the Code of Practice and of his reasons for regarding that information as relevant for that purpose. It must also contain particulars of the rights of appeal conferred by section 57 of the FOIA.

8. Authorities should note that if they are failing to comply with the Code, they may also be failing to comply with the Public Records Acts 1958 and 1967, the Local Government (Records) Act 1962, the Local Government Act 1972, the Local Government (Access to Information) Act 1985 or other record-keeping or archives legislation, and they may consequently be in breach of their statutory obligations.

9. The Public Records Act (NI) 1923 sets out the duties of public record bodies in Northern Ireland in respect of the records they create and requires that records should be transferred to, and preserved by, the Public Record Office of Northern Ireland.

MAIN FEATURES OF THE FOIA

10. The main features of the FOIA are:

   a) a general right of access to recorded information held by a wide range of bodies across the public sector, subject to certain conditions and exemptions. The right includes provisions in respect of historical records which are more than 30 years old.

   b) in relation to most exempt information, the information must nonetheless be disclosed unless the public interest in maintaining the exemption in question outweighs the public interest in disclosure.

   c) a duty on every public authority to adopt and maintain a scheme which relates to the publication of information by the authority and is approved by the Information Commissioner. Authorities must publish information in accordance with their publication schemes. This scheme must specify:

   - classes of information which the public authority publishes or intends to publish;

   - the manner in which information of each class is, or is intended to be, published; and

   - whether the material is, or is intended to be, available to the public free of charge, or on payment.

d) a new office of Information Commissioner and a new Information Tribunal, with wide powers to enforce the rights created and to promote good practice;

e) a duty on the Lord Chancellor to promulgate Codes of Practice for guidance on specific issues;

f) the amendment of the public records system to integrate it with the new right of access under the FOIA.

TRAINING

11. All communications in writing (including by electronic means) to a public authority fall within the scope of the FOIA, if they seek information, and must be dealt with in accordance with the provisions of the Act. It is therefore essential that everyone working in a public authority is familiar with the provisions of the FOIA, the Codes of Practice issued under its provisions, any relevant Memoranda of Understanding, and any relevant guidance on good practice issued by the Commissioner. Authorities should ensure that proper training is provided.

12. In planning and delivering training, authorities should be aware of other provisions affecting the disclosure of information, such as the Environmental Information Regulations 1992 and their successors which, for example, do not require requests to be in writing.

AUTHORITIES SUBJECT TO THE PUBLIC RECORDS ACTS

13. The guidance on records management and on the transfer of public records in the Code should be read in the context of existing legislation on record-keeping. In particular, the Public Records Act 1958 (as amended) gives duties to public record bodies in respect of the records they create. It also requires the Keeper of Public Records to supervise the discharge of those duties. Authorities that are subject to the Public Records Acts 1958 and 1967 should note that if they are failing to comply with the Code, they may also be failing to comply with those Acts.

14. The Public Records Act (NI) 1923 sets out the duties of public record bodies in Northern Ireland in respect of the records they create and requires that records should be transferred to, and preserved by, the Public Record Office of Northern Ireland.

15. The Information Commissioner will promote the observance of the Code in consultation with the Keeper of Public Records when dealing with bodies which are subject to the Public Records Acts 1958 and 1967

and with the Deputy Keeper of the Records of Northern Ireland for bodies subject to the Public Records Act (NI) 1923.

16. If it appears to the Commissioner that the practice of an authority in relation to the exercise of its functions under the FOIA does not conform with that set out in the Code, he may issue a practice recommendation under Section 48 of the Act. Before issuing such a recommendation to a body subject to the Public Records Acts 1958 and 1967 or the Public Records Act (NI) 1923, the Commissioner shall consult the Keeper of Public Records or the Deputy Keeper of the Records of Northern Ireland.

17. The content of this Code has been agreed by the Deputy Keeper of Records of Northern Ireland. Part II , in particular, describes the roles which public record bodies should perform to ensure the timely and effective review and transfer of public records to the Public Record Office or to places of deposit (as defined in Section 4 of the Public Records Act 1958) or to the Public Record Office of Northern Ireland (under the Public Records Act 1958 or the Public Records Act (NI) 1923). For the avoidance of doubt the term 'public records' includes Welsh public records as defined by Sections 116-118 of the Government of Wales Act 1998.

ROLE OF THE LORD CHANCELLOR'S ADVISORY COUNCIL ON PUBLIC RECORDS AND OF THE PUBLIC RECORD OFFICE

18. To advise authorities on the review of public records, the Lord Chancellor, having received the advice of his Advisory Council on Public Records, (hereafter 'the Advisory Council') may prepare and issue guidance. This may include advice on the periods of time for which the Advisory Council considers it appropriate to withhold categories of sensitive records beyond the 30 year period. In Northern Ireland similar guidance shall be issued by the Deputy Keeper of the Records of Northern Ireland following consultation with the Departments responsible for the records affected by the guidance.

19. The Public Record Office will provide support as appropriate to the Advisory Council in its consideration of applications from authorities in respect of public records and in its preparation of guidance to authorities. In Northern Ireland the Public Record Office of Northern Ireland will provide similar support to the Sensitivity Review Group.

CODE OF PRACTICE ON

1) **The Management of Records by Public Authorities**

and

2) **The Transfer and Review of Public Records under the Freedom of Information Act 2000**

The Lord Chancellor, after consulting the Information Commissioner and the appropriate Northern Ireland Minister, issues the following Code of Practice pursuant to section 46 of the Freedom of Information Act.

Laid before Parliament on 20 November 2002 pursuant to section 46(6) of the Freedom of Information Act 2000.

Introduction

1. The aims of the Code are:

   • **to set out practices which public authorities, and bodies subject to the Public Records Act 1958 and the Public Records Act (NI) 1923, should follow in relation to the creation, keeping, management and destruction of their records (Part I of the Code); and**

   • **to describe the arrangements which public record bodies should follow in reviewing public records and transferring them to the Public Record Office or to places of deposit or to the Public Record Office of Northern Ireland (Part II of the Code).**

2. This Code refers to records in all technical or physical formats.

3. Part One of the Code provides a framework for the management of records of public authorities and of bodies subject to the Public Records Act 1958 and the Public Records Act (NI) 1923, and Part Two deals with the review and transfer of public records. More detailed guidance on both themes may be obtained from published standards. Those which support the objectives of this Code most directly are listed at Annex A.

4. Words and expressions used in this Code have the same meaning as the same words and expressions used in the FOIA.

Part I: Records Management

5. FUNCTIONAL RESPONSIBILITY

5.1 The records management function should be recognised as a specific corporate programme within an authority and should receive the necessary levels of organisational support to ensure effectiveness. It should bring together responsibilities for records in all formats, including electronic records, throughout their life cycle, from planning and creation through to ultimate disposal. It should have clearly defined responsibilities and objectives, and the resources to achieve them. It is desirable that the person, or persons, responsible for the records management function should also have either direct responsibility or an organisational connection with the person or persons responsible for freedom of information, data protection and other information management issues.

6. POLICY

6.1 An authority should have in place an overall policy statement, endorsed by top management and made readily available to staff at all levels of the organisation, on how it manages its records, including electronic records.

6.2 This policy statement should provide a mandate for the performance of all records and information management functions. In particular, it should set out an authority's commitment to create, keep and manage records which document its principal activities. The policy should also outline the role of records management and its relationship to the authority's overall strategy; define roles and responsibilities including the responsibility of individuals to document their actions and decisions in the authority's records, and to dispose of records; provide a framework for supporting standards, procedures and guidelines; and indicate the way in which compliance with the policy and its supporting standards, procedures and guidelines will be monitored.

6.3 The policy statement should be reviewed at regular intervals (at least once every three years) and, if appropriate, amended to maintain its relevance.

7. HUMAN RESOURCES

7.1 A designated member of staff of appropriate seniority should have lead responsibility for records management within the authority. This

lead role should be formally acknowledged and made known throughout the authority.

7.2 Staff responsible for records management should have the appropriate skills and knowledge needed to achieve the aims of the records management programme. Responsibility for all aspects of record keeping should be specifically defined and incorporated in the role descriptions or similar documents.

7.3 Human resource policies and practices in organisations should address the need to recruit and retain good quality staff and should accordingly support the records management function in the following areas:

- the provision of appropriate resources to enable the records management function to be maintained across all of its activities;

- the establishment and maintenance of a scheme, such as a competency framework, to identify the knowledge, skills and corporate competencies required in records and information management;

- the regular review of selection criteria for posts with records management duties to ensure currency and compliance with best practice;

- the regular analysis of training needs;

- the establishment of a professional development programme for staff with records management duties;

- the inclusion in induction training programmes for all new staff of an awareness of records issues and practices.

8. ACTIVE RECORDS MANAGEMENT

Record Creation

8.1 Each operational/business unit of an authority should have in place an adequate system for documenting its activities. This system should take into account the legislative and regulatory environments in which the authority works.

8.2 Records of a business activity should be complete and accurate enough to allow employees and their successors to undertake appropriate actions in the context of their responsibilities, to

- facilitate an audit or examination of the business by anyone so authorised,

- protect the legal and other rights of the authority, its clients and any other person affected by its actions, and

- provide authenticity of the records so that the evidence derived from them is shown to be credible and authoritative.

8.3 Records created by the authority should be arranged in a record keeping system that will enable the authority to obtain the maximum benefit from the quick and easy retrieval of information.

Record Keeping

8.4 Installing and maintaining an effective records management programme depends on knowledge of what records are held, in what form they are made accessible, and their relationship to organisational functions. An information survey or record audit will meet this requirement, help to promote control over the records, and provide valuable data for developing records appraisal and disposal procedures.

8.5 Paper and electronic record keeping systems should contain metadata (descriptive and technical documentation) to enable the system and the records to be understood and to be operated efficiently, and to provide an administrative context for effective management of the records.

8.6 The record-keeping system, whether paper or electronic, should include a set of rules for referencing, titling, indexing and, if appropriate, security marking of records. These should be easily understood and should enable the efficient retrieval of information.

Record Maintenance

8.7 The movement and location of records should be controlled to ensure that a record can be easily retrieved at any time, that any outstanding issues can be dealt with, and that there is an auditable trail of record transactions.

8.8 Storage accommodation for current records should be clean and tidy, and it should prevent damage to the records. Equipment used for current records should provide storage which is safe from unauthorised access and which meets fire regulations, but which allows maximum accessibility to the information commensurate with its frequency of use. When records are no longer required for the conduct of current business, their placement in a designated records centre rather than in offices may be a more economical and efficient way to store them.

Procedures for handling records should take full account of the need to preserve important information.

8.9   A contingency or business recovery plan should be in place to provide protection for records which are vital to the continued functioning of the authority.

9. DISPOSAL ARRANGEMENTS

9.1   It is particularly important under FOI that the disposal of records – which is here defined as the point in their lifecycle when they are either transferred to an archives or destroyed – is undertaken in accordance with clearly established policies which have been formally adopted by authorities and which are enforced by properly authorised staff.

Record Closure

9.2   Records should be closed as soon as they have ceased to be of active use other than for reference purposes. As a general rule, files should be closed after five years and, if action continues, a further file should be opened. An indication that a file of paper records or folder of electronic records has been closed should be shown on the record itself as well as noted in the index or database of the files/folders. Wherever possible, information on the intended disposal of electronic records should be included in the metadata when the record is created.

9.3   The storage of closed records awaiting disposal should follow accepted standards relating to environment, security and physical organisation.

Appraisal Planning and Documentation

9.4   In order to make their disposal policies work effectively and for those to which the FOIA applies to provide the information required under FOI legislation, authorities need to have in place systems for managing appraisal and for recording the disposal decisions made. An assessment of the volume and nature of records due for disposal, the time taken to appraise records, and the risks associated with destruction or delay in appraisal will provide information to support an authority's resource planning and workflow arrangements.

9.5   An appraisal documentation system will ensure consistency in records appraisal and disposal. It should show what records are designated for destruction, the authority under which they are to be destroyed and when they are to be destroyed. It should also provide background information on the records, such as legislative provisions, functional

context and physical arrangement. This information will provide valuable data for placing records selected for preservation into context and will enable future records managers to provide evidence of the operation of their selection policies.

Record Selection

9.6 Each authority should maintain a selection policy which states in broad terms the functions from which records are likely to be selected for permanent preservation and the periods for which other records should be retained. The policy should be supported by or linked to disposal schedules which should cover all records created, including electronic records. Schedules should be arranged on the basis of series or collection and should indicate the appropriate disposal action for all records (e.g. review after x years; destroy after y years).

9.7 Records selected for permanent preservation and no longer in regular use by the authority should be transferred as soon as possible to an archival institution that has adequate storage and public access facilities (see Part Two of this Code for arrangements for bodies subject to the Public Records Acts).

9.8 Records not selected for permanent preservation and which have reached the end of their administrative life should be destroyed in as secure a manner as is necessary for the level of confidentiality or security markings they bear. A record of the destruction of records, showing their reference, description and date of destruction should be maintained and preserved by the records manager. Disposal schedules would constitute the basis of such a record.

9.9 If a record due for destruction is known to be the subject of a request for information, destruction should be delayed until disclosure has taken place or, if the authority has decided not to disclose the information, until the complaint and appeal provisions of the FOIA have been exhausted.

10. MANAGEMENT OF ELECTRONIC RECORDS

10.1 The principal issues for the management of electronic records are the same as those for the management of any record. They include, for example the creation of authentic records, the tracking of records and disposal arrangements. However, the means by which these issues are addressed in the electronic environment will be different.

10.2 Effective electronic record keeping requires:

- a clear understanding of the nature of electronic records;

- the creation of records and metadata necessary to document business processes: this should be part of the systems which hold the records;

- the maintenance of a structure of folders to reflect logical groupings of records;

- the secure maintenance of the integrity of electronic records;

- the accessibility and use of electronic records for as long as required (which may include their migration across systems);

- the application of appropriate disposal procedures, including procedures for archiving; and

- the ability to cross reference electronic records to their paper counterparts in a mixed environment.

10.3 Generic requirements for electronic record management systems are set out in the 1999 Public Record Office statement Functional Requirements and Testing of Electronic Records Management Systems. Authorities are encouraged to use these, and any subsequent versions, as a model when developing their specifications for such systems.

10.4 Audit trails should be provided for all electronic information and documents. They should be kept securely and should be available for inspection by authorised personnel. The BSI document *Principles of Good Practice for Information Management* (PD0010) recommends audits at predetermined intervals for particular aspects of electronic records management.

10.5 Authorities should seek to conform to the provisions of BSI DISC PD0008 – *A Code of Practice for Legal Admissibility and Evidential Weight of Information Stored Electronically (2nd edn)* – especially for those records likely to be required as evidence.

Part II: Review and Transfer of Public Records

11.1 This part of the Code relates to the arrangements which authorities should follow to ensure the timely and effective review and transfer of public records. Accordingly, it is relevant only to authorities which are subject to the Public Records Acts 1958 and 1967 or to the Public Records Act (NI) 1923. The general purpose of this part of the Code is to facilitate the performance by the Public Record Office, the Public Record Office of Northern Ireland and other public authorities of their functions under the Freedom of Information Act.

11.2 Under the Public Records Acts, records selected for preservation may be transferred either to the Public Record Office or to places of deposit appointed by the Lord Chancellor. This Code applies to all such transfers. For guidance on which records may be transferred to which institution, and on the disposition of UK public records relating to Northern Ireland, see the Public Record Office Acquisition Policy (1998) and the Public Record Office Disposition Policy (2000).

11.3 In reviewing records for public release, authorities should ensure that public records become available to the public at the earliest possible time in accordance with the FOIA.

11.4 Authorities which have created or are otherwise responsible for public records should ensure that they operate effective arrangements to determine

a) which records should be selected for permanent preservation; and

b) which records should be released to the public.

These arrangements should be established and operated under the supervision of the Public Record Office or, in Northern Ireland, in conjunction with the Public Record Office of Northern Ireland. The objectives and arrangements for the review of records for release are described in greater detail below.

11.5 In carrying out their review of records for release to the public, authorities should observe the following points:

11.5.1 transfer to the Public Record Office must take place by the time the records are 30 years old, unless the Lord Chancellor gives authorisation for them to be retained for a longer period of time (see section 3 (4) of the Public Records Act 1958). By agreement with the Public Record Office, transfer and release may take place before 30 years;

11.5.2 review – for selection and release – should therefore take place before the records in question are 30 years old.

11.5.3 in Northern Ireland transfer under the Public Records Act (NI) 1923 to the Public Record Office of Northern Ireland is normally at 20 years.

11.6 In the case of records to be transferred to the Public Record Office or to a place of deposit appointed under section 4 of the Public Records Act 1958, or to the Public Record Office of Northern Ireland, the purpose of the review of records for release to the public is to:

- consider which information must be available to the public on transfer because no exemptions under the FOIA apply;

- consider which information must be available to the public at 30 years because relevant exemptions in the FOIA have ceased to apply;

- consider whether the information must be released in the public interest, notwithstanding the application of an exemption under the FOIA; and

- consider which information merits continued protection in accordance with the provisions of the FOIA.

11.7 If the review results in the identification of specified information which the authorities consider ought not to be released under the terms of the FOIA, the authorities should prepare a schedule identifying this information precisely, citing the relevant exemption(s), explaining why the information may not be released and identifying a date at which either release would be appropriate or a date at which the case for release should be reconsidered. Where the information is environmental information to which the exemption at Section 39 of the FOIA applies, the schedule should cite the appropriate exception in the Environmental Information Regulations. This schedule must be submitted to the Public Record Office or, in Northern Ireland, to the Public Record Office of Northern Ireland prior to transfer which must be before the records containing the information are 30 years old (in the case of the Public Record Office) or 20 years old (in the case of the Public Record Office of Northern Ireland). Authorities should consider whether parts of records might be released if the sensitive information were blanked out.

11.8 In the first instance, the schedule described in 11.7 is to be submitted to the Public Record Office for review and advice. The case in favour

of withholding the records for a period longer than 30 years is then considered by the Advisory Council. The Advisory Council may respond as follows:

- by accepting that the information may be withheld for longer than 30 years and earmarking the records for release or re-review at the date identified by the authority;

- by accepting that the information may be withheld for longer than 30 years but asking the authority to reconsider the later date designated for release or re-review;

- by questioning the basis on which it is deemed that the information may be withheld for longer than 30 years and asking the authority to reconsider the case;

- by advising the Lord Chancellor if it is not satisfied with the responses it receives from authorities on particular cases;

- by taking such other action as it deems appropriate within its role as defined in the Public Records Act.

In Northern Ireland there are separate administrative arrangements requiring that schedules are submitted to a Sensitivity Review Group consisting of representatives of different departments. The Sensitivity Review Group has the role of advising public authorities as to the appropriateness or otherwise of releasing records.

11.9 For the avoidance of doubt, none of the actions described in this Code affects the statutory rights of access established under the FOIA. Requests for information in public records transferred to the Public Record Office or to a place of deposit appointed under section 4 of the Public Records Act 1958 or to the Public Record Office of Northern Ireland will be dealt with on a case by case basis in accordance with the provisions of the FOIA.

11.10 Where records are transferred to the Public Record Office or a place of deposit before they are 30 years old, they should be designated by the transferring department or agency for immediate release unless an exemption applies: there will be no formal review of these designations.

11.11 When an exemption has ceased to apply under section 63 of the FOIA the records will become automatically available to members of the public on the day specified in the finalised schedule (i.e. the schedule after it has been reviewed by the Advisory Council). In other cases, if the

authority concerned wishes further to extend the period during which the information is to be withheld in accordance with the FOIA, it should submit a further schedule explaining the sensitivity of the information. This is to be done before the expiry of the period stated in the earlier schedule. The Public Record Office and Advisory Council will then review the schedule in accordance with the process described in paragraph 11.8 above. In Northern Ireland, Ministerial approval is required for any further extension of the stated period.

11.12 In reviewing records an authority may identify those which are appropriate for retention within the department, after they are 30 years old, under section 3(4) of the Public Records Act 1958. Applications must be submitted to the Public Record Office for review and advice. The case in favour of retention beyond the 30 year period will then be considered by the Advisory Council. The Advisory Council will consider the case for retaining individual records unless there is already in place a standing authorisation by the Lord Chancellor for the retention of a whole category of records. It will consider such applications on the basis of the guidance in chapter 9 of the White Paper Open Government (Cm 2290, 1993) or subsequent revisions of government policy on retention.

Annex A

STANDARDS ACCEPTED IN RECORDS MANAGEMENT

- **British Standards (BSI)**

BS 4783	Storage, transportation and maintenance of media for use in data processing and information storage
BS 7799	Code of practice for information security management
BS ISO 15489-1	Information and Documentation – Records Management – Part 1: General
BSI DISC PD 0008	Code of practice for legal admissibility and evidential weight of information stored on electronic document management systems
BSI DISC PD0010	Principles of good practice for information management

BSI DISC PD0012   Guide to the practical implications of the Data Protection Act 1998

- Public Record Office standards for the management of public records

The Public Record Office publishes standards, guidance and toolkits on the management of public records, in whatever format, covering their entire life cycle.

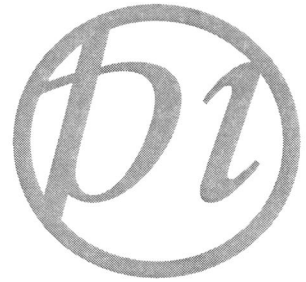

THOROGOOD

PROFESSIONAL

INSIGHTS

Chapter 3

Exemptions and commercial and contract issues

Chapter 3

Exemptions and commercial and contract issues

There are many exemptions from the Freedom of Information Act including for confidentiality reasons. This is very helpful for those who have passed contract and business information to public bodies and are now worried that that information may be disclosed by the public body to a third party, including a competitor in response to a FOIA request. In July 2005 the Government published a review of legislation that prohibits the disclosure of information in response to requests made under the Freedom of Information Act. This found that 210 statutory provisions conflicted with the Act. One of the exemptions under the Act is for legislation, in existence prior to the passing of FOIA, which prohibits the disclosure of information in some way.

Case Example – Exemptions

Case Ref: FS50063659

Date: 12/07/05

Public Authority: Department of Finance and Personnel
Northern Ireland

Summary: The complainant requested details of the full qualifications, experience and duties of each member of the Department's Web Design Team by grade. The public authority withheld information about the full qualifications and experience of each member of the Web Design Team under Section 40 (2) of the FOI Act on the basis that it was personal information and its disclosure would breach the provisions of the Data Protection Act 1998. The ICO is satisfied that public authority has applied the exemption correctly and has dealt with the request in accordance with the requirements of Part 1 of the FOI Act.

Section of the Act/EIR & Findings: FOI s.40 – Not Upheld

At the end of this chapter is a list current at July 2005 of guidance issued by the Information Commissioner.

Part II of the FOIA contains the exemptions as follows preceded by section number:

21. Information accessible to applicant by other means.

22. Information intended for future publication.

23. Information supplied by, or relating to, bodies dealing with security matters.

24. National security.

25. Certificates under ss. 23 and 24: supplementary provisions.

26. Defence.

27. International relations.

28. Relations within the United Kingdom.

29. The economy.

30. Investigations and proceedings conducted by public authorities.

31. Law enforcement.

32. Court records, etc.

33. Audit functions.

34. Parliamentary privilege.

35. Formulation of government policy, etc.

36. Prejudice to effective conduct of public affairs.

37. Communications with Her Majesty, etc. and honours.

38. Health and safety.

39. Environmental information.

40. Personal information. (personal data – see case example above)

41. Information provided in confidence.

42. Legal professional privilege.

43. Commercial interests.

44. Prohibitions on disclosure.

As can be seen there are thus a large number of exemptions. Some are addressed in the Awareness Guidance examined below such as that relating to confidentiality and commercial interests. Indeed, it has been said that if a public body is determined enough it can find an exemption under which to refuse to supply

information. That is going further than is accurate but certainly the exemptions are very broad indeed. There is not space in this report to consider all the exemptions. Those most likely to be relevant in business are considered below.

Commercial and Contract Information and the FOIA

Some of those involved in commercial contracts have been worried about confidentiality of their business documents. The Information Commissioner who enforces the law has issued a set of Awareness Guidance on various topics under the Act (copies of which are attached at the back of this report see www.informationcommissioner.gov.uk – which includes part 5 'Commercial Interest Public Sector Contracts'. This provides considerable help to those concerned about the new rules. The awareness guidance 1 sets out what personal data is caught.

Lots of the tendering processes done by public authorities before the Act were done so on the basis that most, if not all, the information concerning commercial relationships would remain 'confidential'. Often contracts would include confidentiality clauses which purport to prohibit the disclosure of such information. The IC's Office says that "There is clearly concern amongst both public authorities and the private sector regarding the validity of such clauses in existing contracts as well as how information can be protected in the future".

The Act recognises that there are valid reasons for withholding some information in response to a request. The Act lays out 23 situations in which information is considered exempt. **A public authority cannot attempt to contract out of its responsibilities under the Act and unless information is covered by an exemption it must be released if requested**. This is the problem and concern for many businesses – that the FOIA would triumph over confidentiality. This affects existing contracts where the public body already holds the information and new contracts after the 1st January date.

Although any of the 23 exemptions could apply to information concerning the relationship between a public authority and a contractor, the two most relevant exemptions are likely to be section 41, information which has been provided in confidence, and section 43 where the release of information is likely to prejudice someone's commercial interests. Only information that is in fact confidential in nature, or which could prejudice a commercial interest if released, can be withheld under these provisions. It is important that contractors and public

authorities understand what information may be available and how accessibility may change over time.

The Commissioner has also published some awareness guidance which explains the concepts of information provided in confidence and commercial information:

- Awareness Guidance No 2 – Information Provided in Confidence

- Awareness Guidance No 5 – Commercial Interests

There is a separate set on Legal professional privilege – legal advice of which people might request a public body to supply them with copies. Note that *Bowman v Fels (Court of Appeal 8th March 2005)* should be referred to in the guidance on professional privilege, a money laundering case which held that lawyers did not have a duty to report to a special body known as NICS actions of their clients in relation to cases they were litigating, although in other matters they do. There is a conflict between solicitors' duties of confidentiality to their client and their obligation to notify NICS of clients' activities without telling the client. A case is being brought before the European Court of Justice on this under human rights legislation by Belgian lawyers.

The IC's office says:

> "There are a number of points worth noting when applying these exemptions. The commercial interest exemption is subject to a public interest test. That is, public authorities can only withhold commercially sensitive information where the public interest in maintaining the exemption outweighs the public interest in disclosing information. Public authorities should be aware that changing circumstances could strengthen or weaken the public interest arguments in favour of disclosure."

The law of confidence is a common law concept which has been developed by the courts as individual cases are brought before them. This case law will continue to evolve and is likely to be applied by the courts in order to determine what is 'confidential information' under the Act.

The confidential information exemption is not subject to a public interest test under the Act, but under the existing law of confidence it has always been possible to argue that it is in the public interest to make the disclosure. In deciding whether to make a disclosure under the Act, a public authority may look to such case law for guidance. Finally, it should also be remembered that the nature of information will change over time. For example, if information that was once considered confidential subsequently becomes public knowledge it will lose its quality of confidence. Similarly, information that was commercially sensitive

during the tendering process may no longer be sensitive once contracts have been signed, or so says the IC's office.

The Commissioner recognises that public authorities may face some difficult decisions when considering the public interest in disclosing information which it believes could prejudice a third party's commercial interest. When weighing up the public interest it might be appropriate for the public authority to take account of the possible consequences of a third party successfully taking legal action against it following the disclosure of the information. Public authorities should seek their own legal advice in these situations.

It is important that contractors have an understanding that requests may be made for information and that where a request is received information will be disclosed unless it is covered by an exemption. How a public authority raises awareness of its new responsibilities will be for the public authority itself to determine. Some of the clients of the writer's firm have been receiving letters from bodies such as police authorities alerting them to the FOIA's provisions and raising the question of what information they hold from that external contractor might be confidential.

New contracts

At the start of a procurement exercise there will be a number of opportunities for public authorities to inform contractors about Freedom of Information, the guidance says. It will have the option of raising awareness of the Act in its tendering documentation or even at some later stage in the negotiations. Alternatively, the IC is aware that some public authorities intend to refer to their new responsibilities under the Act in the contract. This is something for all readers to consider.

The IC says:

> "One approach would be to identify clearly what information either held in connection with the tendering process, contained in the contract, or the subsequent performance of a contract is commercially sensitive and over what period that information is likely to remain sensitive. Once identified, the information could be listed in a schedule or appendix to the contract. This would have the advantage of providing the contractor with a degree of certainty as to what information is likely to be withheld in response to a request (subject to the public interest test)."

It would also assist the public authority in determining whether an exemption applies within the 20 day time limit allowed.

However, a public authority may decide that it is not practical to identify all of the information which may be commercially sensitive at the outset of a business relationship. Similarly, where it seems unlikely that the contract will ever be the subject of a Freedom of Information request, the public authority may decide that the work involved in trying to identify all such information is not justified.

In these circumstances a public authority may wish to provide a more general assurance to the contractor that commercially sensitive information will be protected (subject to the public interest test). However, such an assurance will only be meaningful if both the public authority and contractor share a proper understanding of how the commercial interest exemption in the Freedom of Information Act operates.

The IC's office says that the disadvantage of this second approach is that the public authority will have more work to do in identifying the commercially sensitive information if it did receive a request. It may, therefore, be sensible to establish a consultation procedure so that if a request was received the contractor could provide advice as to what information would prejudice its commercial interests were it to be released.

"In short, the Commissioner recognises that there is a place for confidentiality clauses where they serve to identify information that may be exempt. That is not to say that the information referred to in such a clause would automatically attract an exemption. The information would still have to be reviewed in light of all the circumstances existing at the time a request was received in order to decide whether or not it could be withheld. The clause would help identify occasions when it would be helpful to consult the contractor."

A confidentiality clause which provides a false sense of security that information can be withheld when it is in fact not covered by an exemption in the Act, will only damage commercial relationships if a public authority decides to release information at a later date. This is a problem for local authorities too.

Even if a clause attempts to prevent the disclosure of information, the disclosure would not lead to an actionable breach of confidence if the information was not in fact confidential. If the information was not confidential it would have to be released under the Act (subject to the application of the other exemptions) even though this may result in an action for breach of contract.

Public authorities will, therefore, need to be very careful when negotiating such clauses. By agreeing to wide definitions of what constitutes 'confidential information' or 'information which may prejudice commercial interests', the public authority may unwittingly place itself in a future dilemma when faced with a request for information covered by such a clause: to breach its statutory obligation or to breach a contract.

What are local authorities doing?

Some have written to suppliers asking them to identify precisely what information is confidential. Others are taking a general view that they will not readily accede to FOIA requests unless clearly they do not fall within any of the exceptions.

Existing contracts

A public authority may have already entered into contracts that include very broad confidentiality clauses. As a result the contractor may expect all information relating to the contract and its commercial relationship with the public authority to remain confidential even where such information would not be exempt under the Act. Such expectations need revising in light of the Act. This is a very real issue for lots of readers who may not want competitors who lost a tender exercise to see that the successful tenderer sent to the buyer.

Practical advice

The IC says:

> "How this is achieved is an organisational matter for the public authority to decide and may depend, in part, on the number of contracts involved and their value. It may not be practical to revisit every past or existing contract. However, a public authority may consider it wise to review high value contracts or other contracts that are likely to attract requests, for example those implementing or relating to controversial policies. When reviewing such contracts public authorities should aim to advise contractors as to the circumstances in which information may be released under Freedom of Information and to establish consultation procedures."

The writer has had some clients asking for advice on letters they have had from public bodies on exactly this point who have written to those with whom they have existing contracts about the FOIA.

By satisfying itself that the release of information will not prejudice the commercial interest of any party, or provide a basis for an actionable breach of confidence and by being open with contractors about its duties under the Act, a public authority can reduce the risk of a significant claim for breach of contract as a result of any disclosure under the Act.

Marcus Turle, solicitor at City law firm Field Fisher Waterhouse, suggests that companies will have limited options when faced with the prospect of information about their business being made public:

> "They can talk to the public authority and hope to persuade it not to disclose information. They can apply for an injunction preventing disclosure. Or they can sue for damages after the event (and perhaps get an injunction to prevent further disclosure in future). Of course, none of these provides certainty of outcome, and the last two will be expensive. What is more, the first and second options will only be available if the public authority actually notifies the company before it responds that it has received a request."

This is an issue many companies are currently grappling with.

He also suggests companies do the following:

1. Find out from public sector customers who their Freedom of Information Champion is, how their records management policies work, and clarify who will bear the costs for producing information which the company might be holding on the customer's behalf (if, for example, the company is an outsourcing service provider).

2. Companies should make sure the contract requires their public sector customers to consult them (or at the very least notify them) before they disclose information about them in response to a FOIA request.

3. Companies should discuss with their customers now (or when negotiating future contracts) what information about the company will and will not be potentially disclosable under FOIA. Ideally, they should put together a list of what is commercially sensitive and a list of other information which they think might fall under one of the other exemptions in FOIA.

What is clear is that taking no action could be risky. The Act is not entirely negative however. Some companies will find it very useful to glean information about

competitors or Government bodies or departments with whom they deal and the aims of the FOIA should not be forgotten – a very long standing Labour Party pledge to ensure open and accessible Government. Canada, Australia, New Zealand and Ireland have had measures similar to this for some years and their experience is useful in assessing the likely impact in the UK.

Wording for contracts

When advising a local authority or other state body client it is worth looking at the recently published Office of Government Commerce IT contracts which are on the internet on the OGC web site. They contain, amongst many other clauses, FOIA/confidentiality provisions which can be of assistance when advising state buyers on what clauses to include in contracts.

The OGC has also published new guidance to support the use of the standard set of terms and conditions.

The two sets of standard terms and guidance can be downloaded from the OGC web site:

http://www.ogc.gov.uk/sdtkdev/new_content/decisionmap/tcintro.html

Further information

The Information Commissioner is in charge of this area – see www.informationcommissioner.gov.uk under Freedom of Information.

Awareness Guidance has been published by the IC in the following areas accessible via the IC's web site – this is regularly updated so always look for the latest information. Some of the guidance is attached to this report in the Appendices:

- Awareness Guidance 1 – Personal Information

- Awareness Guidance 2 – Information provided in confidence

- Awareness Guidance 3 The Public Interest

- Awareness Guidance 4 – Legal Professional Privilege section 42

- Awareness Guidance 5 – Commercial Interest

- Awareness Guidance 5 – Annex Public Sector Contracts

- Awareness Guidance 6 – Information Reasonably Accessible to the Applicant by Other Means

- Awareness Guidance 7 – Information Intended for Future Publication

- Awareness Guidance 8 – Records Management FAQs

- Awareness Guidance 9 – Information contained in court records

- Awareness Guidance 10 – Defence Exemption

- Awareness Guidance 11 – Time for Compliance

- Awareness Guidance 12 – When is information caught?

- Awareness Guidance 13 – Relations within the UK

In addition to the Awareness Guidance series, the Commissioner also has a programme of **policy development** designed to enable him to deal with complaints involving the application of the **exemptions** in the Act and the public interest test. Although the purpose of this policy work is for internal purposes, the Commissioner has decided to make it generally available as an aid to understanding the Act and preparing for implementation.

Guidance currently available on the exemptions includes:

- Audit Exemptions

- Court Records (section 32)

- The Economy (section 29)

Exemptions Guidance

General Principles: List of absolute/qualified exemptions:

Duty to Confirm or Deny	Awareness Guidance 21http: //www.informationcommissioner.gov.uk/cms /Document Uploads/AG 20 Prejudice Adverse Affect.pdf
Prejudice and Adverse Affect	Awareness Guidance 20
Public Interest Test	Awareness Guidance 3

The Exemptions

Relations within the UK – Awareness Guidance 13

Commercial Interest (Section 43)	Awareness Guidance 5 Public Sector Contracts – Annexe
Communications with Her Majesty and the Awarding of Honours (Section 37)	Awareness Guidance 26
Defence (Section 26)	Awareness Guidance 10
Economy (Section 29)	Awareness Guidance 15
Effective Conduct of Public Affairs (Section 36)	Awareness Guidance 25
Health and Safety (Section 38)	Awareness Guidance 19
Information contained in Court Records (Section 32)	Awareness Guidance 9
Information intended for Future Publication (Section 22)	Awareness Guidance 7
Information provided in Confidence (Section 41)	Awareness Guidance 2
Information reasonably accessible to the Applicant by other Means (Section 21)	Awareness Guidance 6
International Relations (Section 27)	Awareness Guidance 14
Investigations (Section 30)	Awareness Guidance 16
Law Enforcement (Section 31)	Awareness Guidance 17
Legal Professional Privilege (Section 42)	Awareness Guidance 4
Parliamentary Privilege (Section 34)	Awareness Guidance No 28 http://www.informationcommissioner.gov.uk/cms/DocumentUploads/AG 1 personal info.pdf
Personal Information (Section 40)	Awareness Guidance 1

Policy Formulation, Ministerial Communications, Law Officers' Advice and the Operation of Ministerial Private Office (Section 35)	Awareness Guidance 24
Prohibitions on Disclosure (Section 44)	Awareness Guidance 27
Public Audit (Section 33)	Awareness Guidance 18
Relations within the UK (Section 28)	

http://www.informationcommissioner.gov.uk/cms/
DocumentUploads/AG 28.pdf

Casework Advice

This has been produced to assist the Commissioner's staff when dealing with complaints that requests for information have not been dealt with properly or that information has been withheld.

Audit Awareness (Section 33)	Casework Advice 3
Court Records (Section 32)	Casework Advice 2
Economy (Section 29)	Casework Advice 1

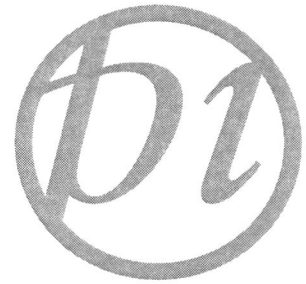

Appendices to this Report

Freedom of Information Act Awareness Guidance No 1

Personal Information

The right under the Freedom of Information Act to request official information held by public bodies under (known as the **right to know**) comes into force in January 2005. The Awareness Guidance series is published by the Information Commissioner to assist public authorities and, in particular, staff who may not have access to specialist advice in thinking about some the issues. Here we look at the exemption relating to personal information. The exemption is set out in section 40 of the Act. The aim of the series is to introduce some of the key concepts in the Act and to suggest the approaches that may be taken in preparing for implementation.

What does the Act say?

Section 40 of the Act sets out what appears at first sight to be a complicated exemption from the **right to know** where the information requested consists of personal data. Fortunately, the exemption is not as difficult as it first appears. It can be summarised as follows:

- If the personal data is about the person requesting the information, then there is no **right to know** under the Freedom of Information Act. There is, in other words, an absolute exemption. However, any such requests automatically become subject access requests under the Data Protection Act and must be treated as such. This means that despite the exemption under the Freedom of Information Act, the applicant has a right to his or her information under the Data Protection Act.

- If the personal data is about someone other than the applicant, there is an exemption if disclosure would breach any of the Data Protection Principles. (This is the main issue explored in this guidance.) There are also some special rules to be applied in cases where the personal data are about someone who has formally objected to their disclosure. The term, "**third party data**," is used to describe personal information about someone other than the applicant.

What is personal data?

The term "personal data" is defined in the Data Protection Act, as amended by the Freedom of Information Act. "Personal data" is information about a living individual from which that individual can be identified. It may take any of the following forms

- Computer input documents;
- Information processed by computer or other equipment (e.g. CCTV);
- Information in medical, social work, local authority housing or school pupil records;
- Information in some sorts of structured manual records;
- Unstructured personal information held in manual form by a public authority.

The last of these categories was introduced into the Data Protection Act by FOI. For public authorities it means that, in effect, any information held about living individuals is potentially accessible under the Freedom of Information Act. However, in the case of this last type, which is sometimes referred to as **category e) data**, there are some special rules designed to reduce the administrative burden which requests for information are likely to place on authorities. These are explained in the next section. For private sector organisations, the definitions in the Data Protection Act are unchanged.

Subject Access Requests

Subject access requests must be made in writing. The definition includes requests made by email. There is no requirement to refer to the Data Protection Act and there will almost certainly be people who request information about themselves (i.e. personal data) while mistakenly citing the Freedom of Information Act. In any event, if the request is for personal data relating to the applicant, it must be treated as a request under the Data Protection Act.

If you calculate that you will be unable to respond within the 20 working day period provided by the FOI Act and that you may need the full 40 calendar day period allowed for under the Data Protection Act, you should let the applicant know.

Under the FOI Act, an applicant must simply state his or her name, provide an address for correspondence and describe the information requested. Only in exceptional circumstances will you be justified in seeking to verify the applicant's identity - for instance if you suspect that a request is a vexatious one, submitted under an assumed name. Under the Data Protection Act, by contrast, you must avoid making disclosures of personal information which would breach the Act. In sensitive cases or where you suspect that the applicant is not who they claim to be, you may therefore need to check signatures or ask for proof of identity.

The usual subject access fee under the Data Protection Act is £10. (Exceptions are a fee of up to £50 for medical records and a sliding scale for school pupil records.) However, where the request is for unstructured personal information, charges can be

made in accordance with the Freedom of Information rules. These will be set out in regulations.

It is also worth remembering, particularly in the case of unstructured information, which may be hard to locate, that public authorities need not respond unless they are given any information which they reasonably need to find the information requested.

The Data Protection Act contains a number of exemptions from the right of subject access. These are explained in the "Data Protection Act 1998 Legal Guidance", also published by the Commissioner. The Commissioner has also published a large amount of information about subject access rights which is available from the data protection area of his web site or may be requested from the Information Line (01625 545 745).

Requests for Third Party Data

The Data Protection Act contains 8 principles which, taken together, form the basic standard to which those processing personal data must operate. When an applicant asks for **third party data**, that request can only be refused if disclosure would breach any of the data protection principles.

The first principle requires personal data to be processed fairly and lawfully. In practice this will be the key issue when considering an application for **third party data**.

Disclosure would be unlawful if:

- There would be a breach of confidence. The duty of confidence is the subject of <u>Awareness Guidance No 3</u>. It is likely to arise where relatively sensitive information has been provided to an authority in the expectation that it would not be disclosed. Examples include medical information or personal financial details.

- There is a law forbidding disclosure, for instance the Official Secrets Act.

The concept of "fairness" is harder to define, although in practice it ought not to be difficult to judge whether it would be unfair to someone to pass on their information without consent. The sorts of questions which should be asked include:

- Would the disclosure cause unnecessary or unjustified distress or damage to the person who the information is about?
- Would the third party expect that his or her information might be disclosed to others?
- Had the person been led to believe that his or her information would be kept secret?
- Has the third party expressly refused consent to disclosure of the information?

Private or Public Lives?

In thinking about fairness, it is likely to be helpful to ask whether the information relates to the private or public lives of the third party. Information which is about the home or family life of an individual, his or her personal finances, or consists of personal references, is likely to deserve protection. By contrast, information which is about someone acting in an official or work capacity should normally be provided on request unless there is some risk to the individual concerned.

While it is right to take into account any damage or distress that may be cause to a third party by the disclosure of personal information, the focus should be on damage or distress to an individual acting in a personal or private capacity. The exemption should not be used, for instance, as a means of sparing officials embarrassment over poor administrative decisions.

An issue which will often arise is whether the Data Protection Act prevents the disclosure of information identifying members of staff. Applying the criteria suggested above, if the information requested consists of the names of officials, their grades, job functions or decisions which they have made in their official capacities, then disclosure would normally be made. On the other hand, information such as home addresses or internal disciplinary matters would not normally be disclosed. While it would be wrong to disclose bank account details of staff, it would be unlikely to be unfair to publish details of expenses incurred in the course of official business, information about pay bands, or, particularly in the case of senior staff, details of salaries. While this information clearly does relate to staff personally, there is a strong public interest in provision of information about how a public authority has spent public money.

These are not hard and fast rules. While names of officials should normally be provided on request, if there is some reason to think that disclosure of even that information would put someone at risk – for instance confirming the work address of a member of staff who has been physically threatened – then it may be right not to give out that information. It may also be relevant to think about the seniority of staff: the more senior a person is the less likely it will be unfair to disclose information about him or her acting in an official capacity.

Formal objections to disclosure

The Data Protection Act gives people the right to object in writing to the processing or disclosure of their personal data. Such written objections are often referred to as **Section 10 Notices.** An organisation receiving such a notice must comply unless there is some overriding justification for the processing. In some cases, although an organisation does not accept that there are valid grounds for objection, it may agree not to process or disclose data simply because those are the wishes of the person concerned.

If a request for the disclosure of information to which the third party has previously objected is received, then, under FOI, the public authority must review its decision to accept the objection and must provide a copy of the information unless it is satisfied that the objection was in fact a valid one.

Key issues in preparing for implementation of the FOI Act

- Many public authorities are used to dealing with subject access requests under the Data Protection Act and with the old definitions of personal data. Staff need to be aware of the fact the definitions have been broadened to include unstructured personal information.

- It is often believed that the Data Protection Act prevents the disclosure of any personal data without the consent of the person concerned. This is not true. The purpose of the Data Protection Act is to protect the private lives of individuals. Where information requested is about the people acting in a work or official capacity then it will normally be right to disclose.

- You should develop a policy as to what information will be routinely disclosed about staff and what might be withheld. Your policy is likely to be more effective and you will avoid unnecessary alarm if this policy is developed in consultation with staff.

Freedom of Information Act Awareness Guidance No 2

Information provided in confidence

The right under the Freedom of Information Act to request official information held by public bodies under (known as the **right to know**) comes into force in January 2005. The Awareness Guidance series is published by the Information Commissioner to assist public authorities and, in particular, staff who may not have access to specialist advice in thinking about some the issues. Here we look at the exemption relating to information subject to a duty of confidence. The exemption is set out in section 41 of the Act. The aim of the series is to introduce some of the key concepts in the Act and to suggest the approaches that may be taken in preparing for implementation.

What does the Act say?

Section 41 of the Act sets out an exemption from the **right to Know** if the information in question was provided to the public authority in confidence. There are two components to the exemption:

- The information must have been obtained by the public authority from another person. A person may by an individual, a company, a local authority or any other "legal entity". The exemption does not cover information which the public authority has generated itself although another exemption may apply (e.g. s.43 where the information may prejudice the commercial interests of the authority itself.)

- Disclosure of the information would give rise to an actionable breach of confidence. In other words, if the public authority disclosed the information the provider or a third party could take the authority to court.

In trying to decide whether information received from a third party falls within this exemption, it may be necessary to think about two questions: "Can the authority disclose the information?" and, "Can the authority confirm or deny the existence of the information?" For instance, a financial regulator might decline to confirm or deny that it has been provided with a confidential report on a company since to confirm that it even held a report would indicate that it harboured suspicions about the activities of that company. However, if it was already public knowledge that a report had been sent to it, there would be no breach of confidence in confirming receipt. In both cases, the regulator might not wish to disclose the content of the report.

What is confidentiality?

A duty of confidence arises when one person (the "confidant") is provided with information by another (the "confider") in the expectation that the information will only be used or disclosed in accordance with the wishes of the confider. If there is a breach of confidence, the confider or any other party affected (for instance a person whose details were included in the information confided) may have the right to take action though the courts.

The law of confidence is a common law concept. This means that rather than an Act of Parliament setting out what is confidential, what is not and the penalties for a breach of confidence, the law in this area has been developed by the courts as individual cases have been brought before them. The common law has strengths, in particular it is flexible and develops over time. It also has some difficulties, for instance it is often necessary to apply the lessons of one case to another which may have very different elements.

For the purposes of FOI, the key issue is likely to be the disclosure rather than the use of information. In trying to determine whether an obligation of confidence has arisen in a particular case, it is likely to be necessary to think first about the circumstances under which information was provided to the authority and second about the nature of that information.

The circumstances under which the information was provided

There are essentially two cases:

- When the confider provides information to the authority, explicit conditions are attached to its subsequent use or disclosure. This may take the form of a contractual term or may be stated, for instance, in a letter.

- Conditions are not stated explicitly but are obvious or implied from the circumstances. For instance a patient does not need to tell a doctor not to pass his or her information on to a journalist: it is simply understood that those are the rules.

The second case is more likely to give rise to some uncertainty since there is always the risk that the expectations of the confider and the confidant may be different. Some of the circumstances which typically give rise to obligations of confidence are reasonably well known. In addition to the patient/doctor relationship, can be added a number of other relationships: client/lawyer, penitent/priest, customer/bank, client/social worker and so on.

Others are more difficult to pin down. For instance employers clearly have obligations of confidence towards their employees although these are not all encompassing. For instance, while it is fairly obvious that information contained in

staff appraisals should not be disclosed, other information such as names and job titles are unlikely to be confidential. If in doubt, it may be sensible to take some advice and to consult whoever may be affected by the requested disclosure of information.

Public authorities that gather information by means of statutory powers, including regulatory and tax collecting bodies, should consider whether the law of confidence (in addition to any statutory prohibitions) would prevent the disclosure of that information to third parties.

The nature of the information

Information which is protected from disclosure by an obligation of confidence must have the necessary "quality of confidence". There are two key elements to this:

- The information need not be highly sensitive. However, nor can it be trivial. The preservation of confidences is recognised by the courts to be an important matter and one in which there is a strong public interest. This notion is undermined if it is argued that even trivial matters are covered.

- The information must not be readily available by other means. Information which has been reported in the press or a chemical formula which can be worked out by any chemical analyst, for instance, are unlikely to be viewed by the courts as being confidential. On the other hand, it is not necessary that the information is completely secret. A patient does not lose the right to medical confidentiality, for instance, simply because he or she has given details of their condition to an employer or a friend.

When can confidential information be disclosed?

The duty of confidence is not absolute and the courts have recognised three broad circumstances under which confidential information may be disclosed. These are as follows:

- Disclosures with consent. If the person to whom the obligation of confidentiality is owed (whether an individual or an organisation) consents disclosure will not lead to an actionable breach of confidence.

- Disclosures which are required by law. "Law" in this context includes statute, rules of law, court orders etc. (Note, however, that if disclosures are requirements of law, it is unlikely that the person seeking the information will attempt to make use of FOIA in order to obtain it.)

- Disclosures where there is an overriding public interest. There are no hard and fast rules here. The important thing to note, however, is that the courts have generally taken the view that the grounds for breaching confidentiality must be strong ones. Confidentiality is recognised as an important thing in itself. In balancing confidentiality against the public interest, the task is not to weigh up the

Final Version 1

3

impact upon the individual against the good of society, but rather the good of society against the importance of preserving confidences. In a medical context, confidentiality is important because is reinforces the bond of trust between patients and doctors, without which people may be reluctant to seek medical advice. In a banking context, confidences are respected in order to maintain trust in the banking system as a whole. Examples of cases where the courts have required disclosure in the public interest include those where the information concerns misconduct, illegality or gross immorality.

"Actionable" breaches of confidence

Public authorities relying upon the exemption must be satisfied that any breach of confidence would be actionable. "Actionable" means that is an aggrieved party would have the right to take the authority to court as a result of the disclosure. There are essentially two considerations.

- The authority must be satisfied the information in question is in fact confidential. If in doubt, it may be necessary to take advice, including from the person affected. In the final analysis, however, the authority itself must be satisfied that an obligation of confidence exists: there is no veto given to third parties who object to disclosure

- The aggrieved party must have the legal standing to take action. The Act makes clear, for instance, that one government department or one Northern Ireland department cannot sue another.

Issues for Implementation

Central government departments (and some other authorities) make use of systems of protective markings (e.g. Restricted, confidential, secret, top secret). While these markings may provide a useful preliminary indication, it would be a mistake to rely upon them to make final decisions. A document may have been marked "confidential" because it was sensitive at the time of creation but is no longer so. Documents may have been generated by the authority itself, and so not be capable of containing information falling within the exemption. If protective marking systems are to be of assistance, it may be necessary to also record the period of time for which the marking is anticipated to be relevant together with any other information that might assist an FOI decision maker.

Similar considerations will apply to information which has been provided to a public authority marked, "Confidential" or "Commercial in Confidence" and so on. Very often such markings do not provide a good indication of whether information has in fact the necessary "quality of confidence". As with internal markings, what was confidential at the time of writing may no longer be at the time of a request for disclosure. It is also quite likely that some information will have been provided to an authority in the expectation that it would not be disclosed, even though no explicit restriction was placed upon it. In all these cases, if in doubt, it will be sensible to check the position

with the provider of the information and any third parties, bearing in mind that it is the authority and not a third party which must decide if the exemption is relevant.

Given the scope for misunderstanding, for instance over the extent of the obligation of confidence in respect of employees, it may be sensible to set out formally the circumstances under which the authority will regard information as confidential. This will alert anyone who wishes to place restrictions upon the use of information of the need to do so explicitly.

The Access Code issued under s.45 of the Act by the Lord Chancellor giving advice on the handling of requests under the Act contains the following passage about contract terms with commercial organisations:

"When entering into contracts public authorities should refuse to include contractual terms which purport to restrict the disclosure of information held by the authority and relating to the contract beyond the restrictions permitted by the Act. Public authorities cannot "contract out" of their obligations under the Act. Unless an exemption provided for under the Act is applicable in relation to any particular information, a public authority will be obliged to disclose that information in response to a request, regardless of the terms of any contract."

Although the focus of this advice is commercial interests, it can apply equally to the authorities faced with decisions as to whether to accept confidentiality clauses. (See also the Commissioner's guidance on the exemption relating to commercial interests, Awareness Guidance No 5)

Other exemptions

The law of confidence (and therefore section 41 of the Act) can present difficulties, particularly to those who do not have access to legal advice. For this reason, it may often be worth considering whether there are any other exemptions in the Act which may be more immediately relevant.

Although relations between government departments and internally generated information cannot be protected by the duty of confidence, it may be relevant to look at, say, the exemptions relating to defence, the economy or prejudice to the effective conduct of public affairs.

Information which a court might find was subject to an obligation of confidence because it had been obtained using statutory powers, may also be protected by the exemptions relating to investigations, law enforcement or audit.

Information about personal finances, health of individuals is protected by the Data Protection Act. S.40 of the Freedom of Information Act is therefore relevant (see Awareness Guidance No 1.)

Freedom of Information Act Awareness Guidance No 3

The Public Interest Test

The right under the Freedom of Information Act to request official information held by public bodies (known as the **right to know**) comes into force in January 2005. The **Awareness Guidance** series is published by the Information Commissioner to assist public authorities and, in particular, staff who may not have access to specialist advice in thinking about some the issues. Here we consider the application of the public interest test when deciding whether to release or disclose information which has been requested. The aim of the series is to introduce some of the key concepts in the Act and to suggest the approaches that may be taken in preparing for implementation.

The public interest lies at the heart of the Freedom of Information Act and readers should note that this guidance is simply a starting point. Further, more comprehensive guidance will be issued by the Commissioner in due course. The guidance should be read in conjunction with <u>Balancing the Public Interest: Applying the public interest test to exemptions in the UK Freedom of Information Act 2000</u>. This booklet, published by the Constitution Unit which was commissioned to produce it by the Information Commissioner, is available in hard copy from the address at the end of this guidance.

A) What does the Act say?

Section 1 of the Act sets out the rights of any person making a request for information to a public authority. These are:

- the right to be informed whether or not the information requested is held by the authority, and, if so,
- the right to have that information communicated to him.

In principle both these rights must be considered separately and, when applying the public interest test, consideration should be given first to whether it is right to confirm or deny the existence of information and second to whether that information should be supplied. In practice, most of the time the two questions will merge and for the purposes of this awareness guidance, the two questions are treated as a single **right to know**.

Section 2 then sets out the circumstances under which a public authority may refuse a request. In broad terms these are as follows:

- Absolute exemptions. These are cases where the right to know is wholly disapplied. In some cases there is no legal right of access at all, for instance information supplied by or relating to bodies dealing with security matters or information covered by parliamentary privilege. In other cases, for instance information available to the applicant by other means or personal information relating to the applicant, it may be possible to obtain the information by alternative means although not under the FOI Act. (The Personal Information exemption is the subject of <u>Awareness Guidance No 1</u>.)

- Qualified exemptions. These are cases where a public authority, having identified a possible exemption, must consider whether there is a greater public interest in confirming or denying the existence of the information requested and providing the information to the applicant or in maintaining the exemption.

Some of the exemptions in the Act are class exemptions and some prejudice based. Class exemptions are designed to give protection to all information falling within a particular category, for instance, information subject to legal professional privilege. Prejudice-based exemptions only come into force if a particular disclosure would prejudice the purpose of the exemption, for instance prejudice to international relations. The important thing to note is that both class and prejudice based exemptions are subject to the public interest test unless the Act states that they are absolute exemptions. All the exemptions are listed in Appendix 1. The public interest only needs to be considered where there is an exemption and that exemption is qualified.

B) What is the "public interest"?

It is often suggested that the fact that the term "the public interest" is not defined in the Act leads to difficulty. This should not be the case. From time to time weighing competing interests may be difficult. However, this does not mean that the nature of the task facing a public authority when applying the public interest test is unclear. In effect something "in the public interest" is simply something which serves the interests of the public. When applying the test, the public authority is simply deciding whether in any particular case it serves the interests of the public better to withhold or to disclose information. The following examples may illustrate the point.
Section 31 of the Act exempts information whose disclosure would, or would be likely to prejudice the prevention or detection of crime or the apprehension or prosecution of offenders.

A request is received by a police force about the relative detection rates for burglaries in different areas of a city. The police may consider that by responding to the request there is some risk that criminals may be able to make use of the information in planning crimes. It is therefore relevant to at least consider the exemption. However, the risk of assistance being given to burglars must be weighed against the general public interest in openness, important aspects of which include promoting accountability and increasing participation in public debate about matters of public policy such as policing.

A second request is for information about the number of police officers allocated to guarding visiting dignitaries. In this case there is the same risk that supplying the information might assist criminals. There is also the same public interest in openness and accountability. However, the police may argue that the risk presented in the second case is considerably stronger than in the first.

C) Things to be ignored when applying the public interest test

The question of where the public interest lies has often been considered by the courts in newspaper cases, particularly where an individual or organisation attempts to prevent publication of a story. The courts have often distinguished between things which are in the public interest from things which merely interest the public. It will be helpful to bear the distinction in mind.

It is also important to bear in mind that the competing interests to be considered are the public interest favouring disclosure against the public (rather than private) interest favouring the withholding of information. There will often be a **private** interest in withholding information which would reveal incompetence on the part of or corruption within the public authority or which would simply cause embarrassment to the authority. However, the public interest will favour accountability and good administration and it is this interest that must be weighed against the public interest in not disclosing the information. Of course, there will be many occasions when public and private interests coincide. For instance there is often both a private and a public interest in the protection of legal professional privilege: a private interest in that the unauthorised disclosure of information held by a solicitor may damage the client, and a public interest, in that it is in the interests of society as a whole that there is access to justice and a fair trial.

It may sometimes be argued that information is too complicated for the applicant to understand or that disclosure might misinform the public because it is incomplete (for instance because the information consists of a policy recommendation that was not followed). Neither of these are good grounds for refusal of a request. If an authority fears that information disclosed may be misleading, the solution is to give some explanation or to put the information into a proper context rather than to withhold it.

D) Factors in favour of the disclosure of information

There is a presumption running through the Act that openness is, in itself, to be regarded as something which is in the public interest. Setting out the considerations for a public authority when adopting or reviewing its publication scheme, the Act requires that

"... a public authority shall have regard to the public interest –
    (a) in allowing public access to information held by the authority, and
    (b) in the publication of reasons for decision held by the authority."

It may be helpful to think about why openness should be regarded as being for the public good. In the Introduction to the Freedom of Information Act 2000, the Commissioner lists the following public interest factors that would encourage the disclosure of information:

- furthering the understanding of and participation in the public debate of issues of the day. This factor would come into play if disclosure would allow a more informed debate of issues under consideration by the Government or a local authority.
- promoting accountability and transparency by public authorities for decisions taken by them. Placing an obligation on authorities and officials to provide reasoned explanations for decisions made will improve the quality of decisions and administration.
- promoting accountability and transparency in the spending of public money. The public interest is likely to be served, for instance in the context of private sector delivery of public services, if the disclosure of information ensures greater competition and better value for money that is public. Disclosure of information as to gifts and expenses may also assure the public of the personal probity of elected leaders and officials.
- allowing individuals and companies to understand decisions made by public authorities affecting their lives and, in some cases, assisting individuals in challenging those decisions.
- bringing to light information affecting public health and public safety. The prompt disclosure of information by scientific and other experts may contribute not only to the prevention of accidents or outbreaks of disease but may also increase public confidence in official scientific advice.

This list is, of course, not exhaustive and there may be other factors which should be taken into account depending upon the request for information. For instance, the disclosure of information may contribute towards scientific advancements, ensure the better operation of financial and currency markets or assist in the access to justice and other fundamental rights.

E) Factors against the disclosure of information

The main factors counting against the disclosure of information are those which are set out in the exemptions themselves. For instance, there is an obvious public interest in national defence, maintaining good international relations and law

enforcement, as in the example in the Box. If disclosure of information would adversely affect these matters, then it is relevant to consider the exemptions to weigh the possible adverse effect of disclosure against the positive benefit of openness.

There may, however, be other, additional factors to take into account once it has been established that at least one of the FOI exemptions has been engaged. Consideration of the European Convention on Human Rights, for instance may lead to the conclusion that information should not be disclosed because it might prejudice the right to a fair trial.

F) Assistance in thinking about the public interest test

A public interest test is by no means an unusual feature in FOI legislation. On the contrary, virtually everywhere there is an FOI Act there is a public interest test. Similar or identical factors to those listed above can be found in the case law from many other countries. For UK public authorities, the most useful case law is likely to be that from other common law jurisdictions, in particular, Australia, Canada, Ireland and New Zealand. Many of the more relevant cases are summarised in the booklet commissioned from the <u>Constitution Unit, Balancing the Public Interest: Applying the public interest test to exemptions in the UK Freedom of Information Act 2000</u>. These cases should not be followed slavishly, not least because there are some important differences in the legislation in different countries. However, until UK case law is developed they are likely to be an invaluable guide as to how the public interest test should be approached.

Hard copies, priced £15.00 can be obtained from

The Constitution Unit
University College London
29-30Tavistock Square
London
WC1H 9QU

Email constitutior@ucl.ac.uk

In a UK context, it will also be important to consider any decisions made by the Parliamentary Ombudsman when considering complaints under the Open Government Code. Although the Code is not statutory and applies to a much smaller number of public authorities, the public interest test applied by the Ombudsman is identical to that required under the Act. Summaries of cases considered by the Ombudsman under the Code can be found at
http://www.ombudsman.org.uk/pca/document/aoi03nj/index.htm

G) Key Issues for Implementation

1.   Attempt to anticipate likely requests. Having done this it will be easier to identify likely exemptions and, therefore the areas in which the question of the

public interest will arise. There are a number of useful steps which public authorities can take, including:

- analysing the requests for comment and other information which you currently receive from the media and thinking about those which have caused you difficulty;
- analysing the areas of activity which currently give rise to complaints: it is likely that many FOI requests will arise in the context of other disputes between public authorities, the public, suppliers etc.;
- holding discussions with stakeholders (whether the press, pressure groups, customers or suppliers)about the sorts of requests they may make. It may be easier to have more open discussions before the **right to know** comes into force;
- mapping functions onto the exemptions. Although the Act contains 23 exemptions, it is highly unlikely that any public authority will need to rely upon more than a few of them.

2. Devise policies as to what matters to refer to decision makers. Identifying the likely types of request for information, the possible exemptions that may be relevant and some of the public interest questions that will arise should facilitate the establishment of appropriate procedures for dealing with requests. In other FOI jurisdictions where FOI requests must be labelled as such, it is common to refer questions of disclosure or non-disclosure to a more senior person referred to as a "decision maker". Requests under FOIA do not have to be labelled. However, careful consideration of the public interest issues that are likely to arise may enable authorities to produce guidance for their staff as to what sorts of requests may be handled locally and which need to be referred to a more senior member of staff.

3. Look at the casework in other jurisdictions. See above for details of cases considered in other jurisdictions and by the Parliamentary Commissioner. The Department for Constitutional Affairs has also established a working group to consider the public interest. Although the focus of this group's work may be on larger public authorities, there are likely to be lessons for all. The DCA guidance is expected to be published in the second part of 2004.

    As will be apparent from this guidance, in many instances the public interest will only be understood in the context of other FOI exemptions. Readers are therefore directed to advice to be published by the Commissioner the on the exemptions in the Act which will contain advice on the public interest test in particular contexts.

4. Aim for a change of culture. FOI is designed to change the default position from **the need to know** to **the right to know**. Embracing the new culture of openness will involve challenging the way in which things have been done in the past. This may involve a review of how protective marking systems are operated in practice, review of the circumstances under which confidentiality clauses are accepted in dealings with private sector suppliers, or taking a fresh look at how the formulation of policy can be opened up to greater public scrutiny. The important point to grasp is that the public interest does not have

a fixed meaning and that FOIA is designed to shift the balance in favour of greater openness. Again it may be helpful to take a rounded view of these issues before individual requests for information are received.

Appendix 1: The exemptions

a) Qualified

- National security (s.24). (This exemption should be read in conjunction with s.23 – "information supplied by, or relating to, bodies dealing with security matters").
- Defence (s 26)
- International relations (s.27)
- Relations within the UK (s.28)
- The economy (s.29)
- Investigations and proceedings (s.30)
- Law enforcement (s.31)
- Audit functions (s.33)
- Formulation of government policy (s.35)
- Prejudice to effective conduct of public affairs (s.36)
- Communications with her Majesty (s.37)
- Health and safety (s.38)
- Some personal information (s.40). (NB this exemption is the subject of Awareness Guidance No 1)
- Legal professional privilege (s.42)
- Commercial interests (s.43)

b) Absolute

- Information accessible by other means (s.21)
- Information intended for future publication (s.22)
- Information supplied by or relating to, bodies dealing with security matters (s.23)
- Court records (s.32)
- Parliamentary privilege (s.34)
- Personal information (s.40). (NB this exemption is the subject of Awareness Guidance No 1)
- Information provided in confidence (s.41). (NB this exemption is the subject of Awareness Guidance No 2)
- Information whose disclosure is prohibited by law (s.44)

Freedom of Information Act Awareness Guidance No 4

Legal Professional Privilege – Section 42

The right under the Freedom of Information Act to request official information held by public bodies under (known as the **right to know**) comes into force in January 2005. The Awareness Guidance series is published by the Information Commissioner to assist public authorities and, in particular, staff who may not have access to specialist advice in thinking about some the issues. Here we look at the exemption relating to information which may be protected by legal professional privilege. The exemption is set out in section 42 of the Act. The aim of the series is to introduce some of the key concepts in the Act and to suggest the approaches that may be taken in preparing for implementation. It is likely to be particularly important in this area that if there is any doubt about whether the exemption applies that legal advice is obtained.

This awareness guidance deals with the English law concept of legal professional privilege as opposed to the Scottish law concept of 'confidentiality of communications', to which section 42 also refers. Although the two concepts have much in common, you are strongly advised to take additional legal advice so far as Scotland is concerned. (It should also be noted that there is a separate FOI Act which applies to Scottish public authorities. For further information contact the Scottish Information Commissioner www.itspublicknowledge.info)

A) General

What does the Act say?

Section 42 sets out an exemption from the **right to know** if the information requested is protected by legal professional privilege and this claim to privilege could be maintained in legal proceedings. The questions of what is privilege, who can claim and who can waive it, are considered later in this awareness guide.

The Act contains two types of exemption: class-based and prejudice-based. For a prejudice-based exemption to apply, it is necessary to consider whether a particular disclosure would be likely to cause prejudice before the exemption can be applied. The legal professional privilege exemption is class based. Therefore, for the exemption to apply, it is not necessary to demonstrate that any 'prejudice' may occur to the professional legal adviser /client relationship if information is disclosed. Rather, it is assumed that the disclosure of even quite trivial information might undermine the relationship of the lawyer and client.

Nevertheless, the exemption from the **right to know** is conditional and can only be relied upon where the public interest in maintaining the exemption outweighs the public interest in disclosing the information. Issues concerning the 'public interest test' are discussed below. (See also Awareness Guidance No 3.)

What is Legal Professional Privilege?

Legal professional privilege is a common law concept developed by the courts rather than one which is set out in an Act of Parliament. There is no attempt to define the term in the FOI Act. Common law concepts, by their very nature, are not defined in statute. The scope of the exemption may change, therefore, as the courts further develop the concept.

The principle is based upon the need to protect a client's confidence that any communication with his/her professional legal adviser (see 'Who is a professional legal adviser' below) will be treated in confidence and not revealed without consent. This is to ensure there is the greatest chance that justice is administered to the client.

Legal professional privilege protects communications between a professional legal adviser and client from being disclosed, even to a court of law. The emphasis should be on communications (for the purposes of FOI this means information rather than documents). Communications include oral as well as written correspondence. FOI is only concerned with 'recorded information' so oral communications, unless recorded, would not be disclosed in response to a request. However, an Employment Tribunal has held that privilege applies to written notes taken by a director of a company documenting the legal advice obtained in a meeting with the company's professional legal advisers.

Legal professional privilege is a different concept to that of the more general 'confidentiality of communications', so where legal professional privilege does not apply the information may still attract other exemptions, in particular 'information provided in confidence' defined in s.41 of the Act. (See Awareness Guidance No 2).

Who is a 'professional legal adviser'?

The term 'professional legal adviser' encompasses a number of different types of legally qualified individuals including both external and in-house lawyers. It will generally be clear who is a 'professional legal adviser'. Examples include qualified solicitors, barristers and licensed conveyancers.

Within the English legal system legal executives may assist solicitors in the provision of legal advice to clients. Increasingly legal executives hold professional qualifications recognised by the Institute of Legal Executives ('ILEX') but this is not always the case. English law makes no formal provision for the scope of privilege to be extended to cover communications between a client and legally qualified legal executive. Whilst this area of law is not settled the ILEX takes the view that, with regard to legal professional privilege, professionally qualified legal executives holding recognised legal qualifications retained by clients for the provision of legal

advice are to be treated in the same manner as solicitors. For the purposes of FOI legal professional privilege exemption the Commissioner agrees with ILEX on this matter.

Professional legal advisers from whom advice is sought, or with whom communications are made, will usually have a good understanding of legal professional privilege and their advice on whether privilege exists in fact should be sought.

Who can claim privilege?

Privilege attaches to the information itself and belongs to the client. It applies in circumstances explained in Section C of this guidance. Although there are circumstances under which a professional legal adviser ceases to be bound by privilege (see "Cases where privilege ceases to exist", below), it cannot otherwise be waived by the professional legal adviser without instructions from the client. The FOI Act will not change this rule and it will continue to be the case that a professional legal adviser may face disciplinary action and could be subject to a civil action if privileged information is unjustifiably disclosed.

B) Categories of legal professional privilege

There are two categories of legal professional privilege:

- Advice privilege – where no litigation is contemplated or pending
- Litigation privilege – where litigation is contemplated or pending

Litigation refers to the taking of a legal action by one party against another in which an issue is being taken to a court of law for a judge or magistrate to decide.

Advice privilege

This category of privilege attaches to communications between a client and its legal advisers, and any part of a document which evidences the substance of such a communication, where there is no pending or contemplated litigation. The information in question must be communicated in a professional capacity. Consequently, not all communications from a professional legal adviser will attract advice privilege. For example, informal legal advice by a barrister friend to an official given by a lawyer acting in a non-legal capacity or advice to a colleague on a line management issue will not attract privilege.

As is the case with medical information or banking information where an obligation of confidentiality arises out of the special relationships between doctors and patients or bankers and customers, legal professional privilege arises from the nature of the relationship between the professional legal adviser and his or her client. Generally the information covered by privilege will have the same characteristics as other confidential information: for instance, it will be of limited availability.

Communication also needs to be made for the principal or 'dominant' purpose of seeking or giving legal advice. This concept also applies to litigation privilege and is discussed below.

Litigation privilege

This category of privilege arises where litigation is contemplated or is in fact underway. When this is the case, privilege attaches to all documents, reports, information, evidence and the like obtained for the sole or dominant purpose of the proposed or on-going litigation. This clearly includes not only the communications between a professional legal adviser and his or her client but also a variety of other documents.

This privilege is wider than advice privilege described above as it includes not only communications between professional legal adviser and client but extends to communications made with third parties. For example, a public authority in preparing for a case requires a third party expert opinion about scientific data in a particular report. A letter is sent from the authority's legal counsel to the expert and the opinion is given. All notes of correspondence, in this example, would attract litigation privilege as would the expert opinion. Any information being relied upon in proceedings would, however, have to be disclosed to the relevant parties through the normal rules of the court under which parties to litigation must disclose the basis of their case to the other side.

C) Establishing the existence of privilege

In deciding whether in fact information is privileged, it is necessary to ask two further questions.

- What is the purpose for which the information was created or communicated? In other words what is its principal or 'dominant' purpose? Known as the 'Purpose Test'.'

- In the case of litigation privilege only, how likely is the prospect of litigation? Known as the 'Likelihood Test'.

The 'Purpose Test'

For legal professional privilege to apply, information must have been created or brought together for the dominant purpose of litigation or the seeking or provision of legal advice.

With regard to 'advice privilege' the dominant purpose of the communication between client and professional legal adviser must be that of seeking or providing legal advice. The determination of the dominant purpose is a question of fact and the answer can usually be found by inspecting the documents in question. It may also

be helpful to consult the professional legal adviser who created the information or the client. Information does not attract privilege simply by being handed to a professional legal adviser amongst other communications. The test is whether the information was passed to a professional legal adviser for the sole or dominant purpose of obtaining legal advice.

The issue of 'dominant purpose' of communications was considered by the Three Rivers (No5) case. The Court of Appeal confirmed that the purpose and scope of advice privilege is to enable legal advice to be sought and given in confidence about legal rights and obligations because this is the subject matter that may form the basis of litigation. The emphasis in this case was on the distinction between advice regarding presentational issues, and thus not privileged, and advice concerning the substantive rights and obligations of the Bank, which was privileged.

For example, a local authority social service department conducts a case conference, between a range of professional organisations, to discuss strategies for dealing with a particular issue. An in-house lawyer is invited to these proceedings. The dominant purpose of this conference is not to seek advice about legal rights and obligations but rather to seek a way forward on a particular issue. It is unlikely that information collected at this meeting would attract advice privilege.

With regard to 'litigation privilege' the information must have been created for the purpose of on-going litigation or contemplated litigation. Again, inspection of the documents will often reveal the dominant purpose although occasionally the answer will not be clear-cut. There are occasions where individual pieces of information were created before any litigation was anticipated or commenced. However, a claim for litigation privilege can still be made if those pieces of information have been brought together with others for the purpose of litigation. In general, where the professional legal adviser has exercised skill and judgement in selecting information and not simply copied information wholesale or inserted irrelevant information, a claim for privilege is likely to be upheld by a court.

The 'Likelihood Test' – only applies to Litigation Privilege

For information to attract litigation privilege it must have been created or brought together for the purposes of litigation or anticipated litigation. The courts have ruled that there must be a 'reasonable prospect of litigation' at the time of the information was created or brought together.

It has been held in law that 'litigation cannot be anticipated until a cause of action, or part of it, has arisen'. This includes cases where there is a reasonable prospect that such a cause may arise. For example, a local authority may receive a notice that a pressure group intends to disrupt a peaceful march through its city centre. Any advice which it sought or obtained as to what legal action to pursue in the event of disruption might attract litigation privilege even though the "cause of action" had not yet occurred.

The effect of copying or sharing information

Information may cease to be privileged if it is copied and shared with third parties. The question here will be how widely any copies have been distributed. For example, a local authority, in taking legal proceedings, compiles a report which is afforded the protection of litigation privilege. Where this is copied and sent internally to a selected few, and accordingly retains its confidentiality, the copy will be afforded the protection of privilege. By contrast if the local authority copied and used the report externally, for example, as part of commercial dealings, privilege would be likely to be lost.

A consideration of who is the client will also be relevant here. The client may not include every employee of a large organisation but may be confined to an identifiable team within such a body. If the client is deemed to be a large team, or even a department of a public authority, then the information will be likely to remain privileged if copied amongst this large number of people.

There will be cases in which a public authority holds information subject to privilege owed to a third party. For instance a NHS Trust may have been provided, on a confidential basis, with a copy of legal advice obtained by a Health Authority. In this example the NHS Trust are not owed the privilege and so therefore are not able to waive it. While it would certainly be possible to analyse such cases with reference to the concept of legal professional privilege, it may be simpler to consider the question of confidentiality. (See also Awareness Guidance No 2 on Information Provided in Confidence.)

Cases where privilege ceases to exist

Privilege exists in order to advance justice. It does not apply to information that conceals fraud, crime or the innocence of an individual. Loss of the privilege occurs even where the professional legal adviser is unaware of the wrongdoing. Advice warning a client about the danger of prosecution would normally attract privilege since the fraud or crime has yet to be committed but once a professional legal adviser becomes aware of the wrongdoing the associated information ceases to be privileged. Furthermore, a distinction must be drawn between legal advice given after a wrongdoing has been committed, which would normally attract privilege, and advice given with the intention of furthering a criminal purpose before a wrongdoing, which does not.

D) The 'Public Interest Test'

The legal professional privilege exemption is subject to the public interest test. (See also Awareness Guidance 3 which gives some general advice on this subject.) As explained earlier, the Act cannot be used to force professional legal advisers to disclose privileged information without the consent of the clients to whom the privilege belongs.

The concept of legal professional privilege contains its own built-in public interest test. The privilege may not be claimed where communications are made with a professional legal adviser with the intention of furthering a criminal purpose or are directed to the commission of a crime or fraud.

The Act broadens the scope of consideration of the public interest beyond preventing that which is unlawful to weighing the public interest in disclosing communications and not disclosing them. The Act can, however, be used to oblige an authority with a claim to legal professional privilege to review its decision to maintain the privilege on public interest grounds. All requests must be judged on their own merits. This section of the guidance discusses some of the public interest considerations that will influence a public authority's decision to waive or to maintain its privilege.

Timing of disclosure

Where legal advice has served its purpose, litigation has ended or the possibility of litigation has ended the public authority may be more inclined to disclosure. Although legal privilege could still be claimed, there may be a stronger public interest argument in favour of disclosure particularly if, in fact, no harm would be created. Insofar as the legal advice had been supported by a court and there is no likelihood of appeal, it may be in the public interest to make the full advice more available.

By contrast, where litigation is ongoing and where its disclosure would undermine the prospects of success by the authority, there will be very strong arguments against disclosure.

Legal privilege has classically been applied to information in perpetuity. Under FOI, this is no longer the case and the exemption cannot be applied to information which is deemed to part of a 'historical record', defined in the Act as a record which is 30 years old. In the past privileged documents held by public authorities would have been subject to the National Archives' 30 year rule disclosure provisions, and if extended disclosure was sought an application for extended disclosure was made to the Advisory Council on Public Records. With the implementation of the FOI Act, if it is anticipated that harm may still occur after 30 years by being disclosed, and that harm is real, then other exemptions must be sought in order to protect the information.

Policy Advice

Legal departments and professional legal advisers are becoming increasingly involved in policy development the disclosure of such communications would allow individuals to understand the reasons for decisions made by the respective authority. This was implicitly acknowledged by the High Court in Three Rivers District Council v Bank of England (No10) which considered the advice sought by the client team of the Bank as 'presentational assistance' rather than advice sought about 'the Banks substantive rights and obligations which might in due course be the subject matter of adversarial litigation'. Similarly, policy advice from professional legal advisers not about the substantive rights and obligations of an authority should not be considered privileged.

Traditionally this 'advice' could be considered as protected by legal professional privilege and so not disclosed. One of the themes of the Act is to make public 'reasons for decisions' made by an authority and the Information Commissioner would expect public authorities to re-consider this position in the light of this developing case law and the new environment of openness. In making its decision, the authority will have to weigh up the significance of its decision, including the number of people affected, the public interest in promoting public debate and increasing accountability, against the importance of maintaining the privilege.

Access to justice and the right to a fair trial

Legal professional privilege is one of the guarantees of a fair trial and as such there are powerful public interest arguments in support of not waiving privilege in many cases. The Commissioner would not expect privilege to be waived in cases where disclosure might prejudice the rights either of the authority itself or any third party to obtain access to justice.

Interaction with other FOI exemptions

Legal advice will often contain confidential information about third parties. Under the Act there is an absolute exemption in respect of information whose disclosure would give rise to an act onable breach of confidence. (See also Awareness Guidance No 2 on Information Provided in Confidence.)

Where privileged information contains personal data relating to third parties for instance litigants or witnesses, then it will generally be unfair to those third parties to disclose information. (See also Awareness Guidance No 1 on Personal Information.)

Many public authorities have investigative or law enforcement functions. In cases where disclosure would fall within either the investigations and proceeding or law enforcement exemptions (s. 30 and s.31) of the Act, it may be simpler to apply those exemptions than the legal professional privilege exemption.

E) Issues for implementation

The law on legal professional privilege is complex. This Awareness Guidance does not attempt to deal with all the issues. It is intended to draw attention to the commonly encountered issues in the application of legal professional privilege by the courts.

- As noted above, legal professionals are increasingly involved in providing policy advice. Where this occurs on a regular basis, it may simplify the process of responding to requests for information if a system of marking legal and non-legal advice given by legal staff.

- FOI staff should make all professional legal advisors aware that information 'held' by the authority is subject to FOI and as such any advice given by them may be released at some time in the future.

- It may be helpful to structure legal advice given in particular cases in order to separate information which should not be disclosed, for instance information where disclosure would prejudice the right to a fair trial or the chances of the authority bring a successful prosecution, from more general advice whose publication would increase the public understanding of the reasons for decisions made by the authority.

- Authorities that have significant regulatory or law enforcement functions may wish to consider whether there is general legal advice which they have obtained in the past whose publication might increase public understanding of their policies and practices.

- FOI officers should agree policies with the legal teams of public authorities for when and how to apply the exemption. It would be likely to increase public understanding of decisions to refuse requests if criteria were made public, for instance through the authority's publication scheme.

Freedom of Information Act Awareness Guidance No 5

Commercial Interests

The right under the Freedom of Information Act to request official information held by public bodies under (known as the Right to Know) comes into force in January 2005. The Awareness Guidance series is published by the Information Commissioner to assist public authorities and, in particular, staff who may not have access to specialist advice in thinking about some of the issues. The aim is to introduce some of the key concepts in the act and to suggest the approaches that may be taken in preparing for implementation. Particularly for central government departments (but also for other larger public authorities) more detailed advice on the scope and approach to be taken to the exemption relating to commercial interests will be available from the Department for Constitutional Affairs which is committed to preparing advice on the key exemptions for Whitehall Departments. The Commissioner also intends to issue further advice over the course of 2004.

A) What does the act say?

Section 43 of the Act sets out an exemption from the right to know if:

- the information requested is a trade secret, or

- release of the information is likely to prejudice the commercial interests of any person. (A person may be an individual, a company, the public authority itself or any other legal entity.)

Where the information requested constitutes a trade secret, there is no need to consider the harm its release may cause. The very fact that the information is a trade secret is reason enough to withhold the information (subject to the public interest test). Information which does not constitute a trade secret can only be withheld under this exemption if the public authority is satisfied that to release the information would damage someone's commercial interests. This is referred to as the prejudice test.

The Duty to Confirm or Deny

The "right to know" really refers to two rights. The Act provides that in responding to a request for information a public authority is obliged to inform the applicant whether it holds the information (known as "the duty to confirm or deny"), and if so to communicate it to them. In relation to trade secrets, section 43 does **not** remove the

Final Version 1

1

obligation to inform an applicant whether it holds the information that constitutes the trade secret.

By contrast, where the information requested is likely to prejudice commercial interests other than trade secrets, section 43 not only provides an exemption from the obligation to communicate the information to the applicant but can also provide an exemption from the requirement to inform the applicant whether the information is held. However a public authority can only refuse to confirm or deny whether it holds such information where this in itself would prejudice commercial interests.

The Public Interest Test

This is a qualified exemption. That is, it is subject to the public interest test which is set out in section 2 of the Act. Even where a public authority is satisfied that the information requested is a trade secret or that its release would prejudice someone's commercial interests it can only refuse to provide the information if it believes the public interest in withholding the information outweighs the public interest in disclosing it. Clearly the bias is in favour of disclosure and there will be occasions where information is released even though it is a trade secret or is likely to prejudice someone's commercial interest.

The public interest test is dealt with in more detail in Section D below and in **Awareness Guidance No 3 – The Public interest Test**. Generally speaking, the public interest is served where access to the information would;

- further the understanding of, and participation in the debate of issues of the day;
- facilitate the accountability and transparency of public authorities for decisions taken by them;
- facilitate accountability and transparency in the spending of public money;
- allow individuals to understand decisions made by public authorities affecting their lives and, in some cases, assist individuals in challenging those decisions;
- bring to light information affecting public safety.

In considering the public interest it may also be helpful to bear in mind that certain considerations will not be relevant. For instance, if information is complex or incomplete and therefore potentially misleading these factors should not, in themselves be used to justify non-disclosure. Information should be disclosed if the only likely harm would be embarrassment to the authority although if disclosure might discourage openness in expression opinions, then that might be a reason for withholding it. It may also be necessary to disregard previous requests: the fact that the public interest may not favour disclosure today does not mean that it would not do so given changed circumstances in the future.

B) Trade Secrets

General

Disclosure of a trade secret would, by definition, prejudice a commercial interest. In one respect, however, the Act treats trade secrets differently than other information whose disclosure might harm a commercial interest in that whether or not it is decided to disclose, the public authority must always confirm or deny that it holds the information.

The term "trade secret" is not defined in the Act although it is one which is not difficult to understand. Perhaps the most important thing to grasp is that the term can have a fairly wide meaning. Many people often think of a trade secret to be secret formulae or recipes. While such information is certainly likely to be included in the term, it may also extend to names of customers and the goods they buy or a company's pricing structure if these are neither generally known and the source of a company's "competitive edge". Many of the cases considered by the courts have concerned an employer's ability to prevent the use of information about his business being used by an ex-employee.

In attempting to decide whether information is, in fact a trade secret it may be helpful to ask a number of questions including:

1. Is the information used for the purpose of trade? Information may be commercially sensitive without being the sort of secret which gives a company a "competitive edge" over its rivals. For instance a public authority may hold information about the state of repair of a manufacturer's equipment. While information about the design of the equipment may constitute a trade secret, information about its state of repair would not (even though it may be commercially sensitive) since it is not information which is used to help generate profits.

2. Is it obvious from the nature of the information or, if not, has the owner made it clear that he or she considers releasing the information would cause them harm or be advantageous to their rivals? In considering cases involving former employees, the courts have often found that the question of whether or not the employee knew that disputed information was a trade secret was important.

3. Is the information already known? It may be a statutory requirement for the information to be published in some form (land registry, company house, European Procurement regulations etc). The information may already be common knowledge in the business community. If the information is known beyond a narrow circle, it is unlikely to constitute a trade secret.

4. How easy would it be for competitors to discover or reproduce the information for themselves? Generally the less skill, effort, or innovation that was required to generate the information in the first place, the less likely the information is to constitute a trade secret. By the same token, the easier it would be for a competitor to recreate or discover that information through his own efforts, the less likely it is to be a trade secret.

As we explain in Section E of this guidance, unauthorised disclosures of trade secrets, just as with other breaches of confidentiality, may result in legal action being taken against public authorities. While the Act strongly encourages openness it does not encourage recklessness and, if in doubt, authorities and FOI officers may wish to seek legal advice.

C) Commercial interests

a) General

Trade secrets are one example of commercial interests. The concept is, however, far wider. A commercial interest relates to a person's ability to successfully participate in a commercial activity, i.e. the purchase and sale of goods or services.

The underlying motive for these transactions is likely to be profit, although this is not necessarily the case, for instance where a charge for goods or the provision of a service is made simply to cover costs.

While the essential feature of commerce is trading, the information which falls within the exemption may relate only indirectly to the activity of buying and selling. For instance it is the duty of an employer proposing to make over 100 employees redundant within 90 days to inform the DTI. While this information does not relate directly to a commercial activity, it is easy to see how its disclosure would be likely to undermine a trading position (by making prospective customers less willing to place orders or a bank less likely to extend credit).

There is an important distinction to be drawn between commercial interests and financial interests. While there will be many cases where prejudice to the financial interests of a public authority may affect its commercial interests, this is not necessarily the case. For example, information as to how the level at which Council Tax is set will be information which affects the financial interests of the council, that information does not relate to its commercial activity. Similarly, information concerning central government funding of a local initiative would not be considered commercial information even though there may be competition for the award of grants. There may be grounds under the Act for refusing requests for information as to future levels of Council Tax or central government funding for local initiatives. However the exemption relating to commercial interests is not one of these.

b) Types of Information that may affect Commercial Interests

It may be helpful to consider some of the reasons why a public authority possesses commercial information. This list is only indicative and there may be other circumstances in which a public authority holds such information.

- **Procurement** – public authorities are major purchasers of goods and services and will hold a wide range of information relating to the procurement process. This could be future procurement plans, information provided during a tendering process, including information contained in unsuccessful bids right through to the details of the contract with the successful company. There may also be details of how a contractor has performed under a contract. Further discussion of the issues around procurement information is provided later when considering implementation issues.

- **Regulation** – public authorities may be supplied with information in order to perform their regulatory functions e.g. the issuing of licences. Alternatively they may obtain commercial information whilst investigating potential breaches of regulations that they are responsible for.

- **Public authority's own commercial activities** – some public authorities, for instance publicly owned companies, are permitted to engage in commercial activities. Any information held in relation to these will potentially fall within the scope of the exemption.

- **Policy development** – during the formulation or evaluation of policy a public authority may seek information of a commercial nature. For example in developing a policy aimed at promoting a particular industry a public authority may solicit information from companies in that sector.

- **Policy Implementation** – e.g. policy of encouraging economic development via awarding grants, public authority will hold information in relation to the assessment of the business proposals when awarding those grants.

- **Private Finance Initiative/Public Private Partnerships** – the involvement of private sector partners in the financing and delivering of public sector projects and services has become a common feature of public life. In this context public authorities are likely to hold a good deal of information both related to the particular project in which a private partner is involved and more generally to the private partner's business.

It is important to note that the list above is only refers to *how* a public authority, in the exercise of its functions, may come to hold information relating to business. It does not imply that all such information would be exempt. In order to apply the exemption it is necessary to consider whether the release of such information would *prejudice* someone's commercial interests, i.e. it is necessary to apply the test of prejudice. It will then be necessary to apply the public interest test.

c) The Test of Prejudice

When deciding whether the release of information would, or would be likely to, harm someone's commercial interests it will be necessary to properly consider all the circumstances in question. For example whether the price of goods is commercially sensitive will depend on a number of factors. Releasing information on the price of goods purchased from a catalogue that was freely available to all would not be prejudice the supplier's commercial interests. The price submitted by a contractor is likely to be commercially sensitive during the tendering process but less likely to be so, once the contract has been awarded. In light of this it could be misleading to try and present an incicative list of the sorts of information likely to prejudice someone's commercial interest. A preferred approach is to suggest some of the questions that should be considered in order to determine the impact that releasing the information would have.

1. Does the information relate to, or could it impact on a commercial activity?
As discussed above there is a distinction between commercial interests and financial interests. Commercial information relates to the activity of buying or selling goods and services.

Some information may have a very direct relationship with commercial activity e.g. the price at which goods are offered for sale. Other information may have a less direct link to a commercial transaction, for example, information that a company is considering relocating may have repercussions for labour relations which the company would wish to manage properly in order to minimise disruption to production.

2. Is that commercial activity conducted in a competitive environment?
The level of competition within an industry will effect whether the release of information will harm someone's commercial interests. Where a company enjoys a monopoly over the provision of the goods or services in question it is less likely that releasing the information will have a prejudicial impact on that company.

Alternatively some public authorities may be the sole purchasers of specialist equipment for example military hardware or medical supplies. In such situations the commercial interests of the company could be more dependent on the procurement plans of the public authority in question rather than the effect of releasing commercial information.

3. Would there be damage to reputation or business confidence?
There may be circumstances where the release of information held by a public authority could damage a company's reputation or the confidence that customers, suppliers or investors may have in a company. It may be that releasing such information has a significant impact on revenue or threatens its ability to obtain supplies or secure finance. In these circumstances the commercial interest exemption may be engaged. However it should be noted that there is no exemption for embarrassment, only where there is a real risk of such harm being caused could the exemption be engaged.

4. Whose commercial interests are affected?

In many cases it will be clear whose commercial interests may be prejudiced by a disclosure of information however in other circumstances more thought may be required to identify the stakeholders. Could the release of information operate to the disadvantage of the public authority, for instance by disclosing the budget set aside for a purchase, would this encourage suppliers to raise their prices? Could the information prejudice the bargaining position of the public authority? Will the information impact on the commercial interests of a contractor's suppliers or investors.

5. Is the information commercially sensitive?

Companies compete by offering something different from their rivals. That difference will often be the price at which the goods or services can be delivered but that difference may also relate to quality or specification. Information which identifies how a company has developed that unique element is more likely to be commercially sensitive. For example where a company competes on price, it may be that the final price charged is readily available, however information disclosing how the company is able to offer the product at that price may not be. That is information revealing profit margins is more likely to be commercially sensitive. This argument can extend to working practices etc that allow a quality of service to be more efficiently delivered.

6) What is the likelihood of the prejudice being caused?

Deciding whether or not a particular disclosure would be likely to cause prejudice will often require the exercise of judgement. It will be necessary to judge, in other words, what may be the nature of the harm that would be caused and, also, the likelihood of that harm.

While the "prejudice" that may be caused by disclosure may not be substantial, nor should it be completely trivial. As for likelihood, while prejudice need not be certain, there must be a significant risk rather than a remote possibility of prejudice.

D) The Public Interest

Whether the information requested forms a trade secret or relates to another type of commercial interest, a public authority considering relying upon the section 43 exemption must consider whether there is, in fact an overriding public interest in providing the information. In practice this is likely to involve weighing the prejudice caused by possible disclosure against the likely benefit to the applicant and the wider public.

a) General public interest factors

The factors discussed here are not the only ones that should be considered. However, they illustrate the sort of approach that public authorities should take. Although there is a strong public interest in openness, this does not necessarily override all other considerations.

1. Accountability for the spending of public money

Clearly there is a public interest in allowing scrutiny of how public money is spent. This will be equally true whether a public authority is purchasing goods or services or responsible for awarding grants to private sector companies. Transparency of decisions on how public funds are spent will also generate confidence in the integrity of the procedures involved.

Where a public authority is purchasing goods or services there is a public interest and in ensuring they get value for money. This is particularly true at a time when there is a public debate around the increasing role private companies have in delivering public services.

2. Protection of the public

In the course of its role as a regulator, a public authority may hold information on the quality of products or on the conduct of private companies. There would be strong public interest arguments in allowing access to information which would help protect the public from unsafe products or unscrupulous practices even though this might involve revealing a trade secret or other information whose disclosure might harm the commercial interests of a company.

3. Circumstances under which the public authority obtained the information

Where a public authority obtained information using statutory powers, the disclosure of that information may not prejudice the obtaining of similar information in the future. (Before making a disclosure, however, authorities should also consider whether they are prevented from doing so by the legislation used to obtain the information or by a duty of confidence.)

On other occasiors, the information may have been volunteered to the authority, for instance in the course of research being conducted by the authority. The general presumption in favour of disclosure would have to be carefully weighed against the risk of discouraging private companies from participating in research in the future.

4. Competition issues

There is a public interest in ensuring that companies are able to compete fairly. There is also a public interest in ensuring that there is competition for public sector contracts. In considering the release of information, authorities should therefore take these issues into account, including any reputational damage that disclosure might cause.

Policies on say industrial regeneration, may be implemented through a scheme offering assistance to private companies. Before making a grant to a company a "health check" may be carried out by the authority sponsoring the scheme. Companies may be discouraged from participating in the scheme if they felt it could result in the disclosure of information relating to their general business. In this example, although the public interest would not be served by reducing the participation in the scheme, there is also a public interest in understanding the circumstances in which public money is provided to private companies.

Public authorities should be wary of accepting arguments that the potential for commercial information to be released would reduce the number of companies willing to do business with the public sector, leading to reduced competition and increased costs. In practice, many companies may be prepared to accept greater public access to information about their business as a cost of doing business with the public sector.

Increasing access to information about the tendering process may in fact encourage more potential suppliers to enter the market. A better understanding of the process, the award criteria, knowledge of how successful bids have been put together, could also lead improved bids being submitted in the future. This will lead to more competition and so decrease costs to the public authority. Indeed where a contract comes up for renewal limiting this kind of information is likely to favour the current contractor and so may be anticompetitive.

b) Timing

Very often, in a commercial environment, the timing of the disclosure will be of critical importance. The application of any exemption has to be considered in the circumstances that exist at the time the request is made. Circumstances may change over time. Take the example of information submitted during a tendering process. That information is more likely to be commercially sensitive whilst the tendering process is ongoing compared to once the contract has been awarded. Simply because a request was refused at one point in time does not mean that the information can be permanently withheld. Market conditions will change and for example information relating to costs may very quickly become out of date.

E) Overlap between Commercial Interest and Confidentiality

Many of the exemptions in the Act overlap with others. For instance, disclosure of information about held by one of the armed forces about a defence contract may cause prejudice to national security (s.24), defence (s.26), international relations (s.27) as well as to commercial interests.

Very often, as in this example, the commercial interests exemption will overlap with that relating to information provided in confidence. (*Awareness Guidance No 2* discusses confidentiality in greater detail.) In practice, an indication of whether of not the disclosure of information would in fact cause prejudice to the commercial interests of a third party may be answered by considering the likelihood of the third party being able to successfully take action in the courts for breach of confidence. If the action is successful, the court is likely to award damages in proportion to the commercial loss suffered as a result of disclosure.

Given the financial risk to the authority of breaches of confidence, it may be doubly important for FOI officers to seek legal advice if in doubt.

F) Implementation Issues.

a) Consultation

In order to determine whether the disclosure of information would prejudice a commercial interest, a public authority may wish to consult with the parties likely to be affected by any disclosure. Time is, however, likely to be limited since the public authority must decide whether the exemption applies within 20 working days. A failure by those being consulted to respond does not remove the obligation to respond within that time limit. It may be helpful therefore to have some discussions now with major suppliers and contractors as to the types of information whose disclosure they would consider might harm their commercial interests. It may also be helpful to agree the circumstances under which the public authority will consult in the event of requests in the future.

(Although public authorities may wish to consider the views of the affected party, it is the responsibility of the public authority to decide whether or not the exemption applies. The public authority can only withhold information if is satisfied that any arguments for withholding the information are justified.)

b) Review of Contracts/Confidentiality Clauses

As noted above, there will often be an overlap between section 43 and section 41 which provides that information is exempt where its release could lead to a public authority being taken to court for a breach of confidence.

During the procurement process public authorities may be asked by contractors to accept confidentiality clauses which attempt to prevent the disclosure of information. In many cases such clauses may be perfectly proper and serve to make clear that information which the supplier considers should not be made public and that which can be freely disclosed. Clauses may also be helpful in providing a framework for redress in the event of an unauthorised disclosure.

There is, however a risk, that blanket clauses are proposed which purport to restrict the disclosure of all information including that which could be disclosed without any prejudice to the commercial interests of the supplier. Unless confidentiality clauses are necessary or reasonable, there is a real risk that, in the event of a complaint, the Commissioner would order disclosure in any case. On the other hand, if the issue is properly addressed as contracts are negotiated, confidentiality clauses may prove of real assistance in identifying prejudice to a third party's commercial interests.

In addition to developing a new approach to confidentiality clauses in the future, authorities may also wish to review their existing contracts and to discuss with suppliers and contractors the circumstances under which information might be released in response to a request for information.

Public authorities should also be aware of the Lord Chancellor's Code of Practice under section 45 of the Act. This sets out the standards public authorities are expected to meet in order to comply with their obligations under Part 1 of the Act. It is available from the Department of Constitutional Affairs' website at

http://www.dca.gov.uk/foi/codepafunc.htm.The code discusses public sector contracts and consultation with third parties in more detail.

c) Environmental Information Regulations

The Environmental Information Regulations 1992, which are currently in force, are expected to be replaced by new regulations as from January 2005. A draft of the proposed new regulations is available from the Department for Environment, Food and Rural Affairs' website. Where an application is made for environmental information, the request should be considered under the Regulations rather than the FOI Act.

As currently drafted, the regulations provide an exception from the right of access for information which although broadly similar to the commercial interests exemption in the Freedom of Information Act does not exactly mirror section 43. For instance:

- The exception in the Environmental Information Regulations does not apply to commercial information concerning emissions, discharges and other releases.
- While the commercial interests protected under the FOI Act may include those of the public authority itself, the Regulations are likely only to protect those of third parties.
- The Regulations also include an exception which allows information volunteered to a public authority to be withheld if its release would prejudice the likelihood of such information being provided in the future.

The definition of environmental information is very wide and it would be sensible for all public authorities to familiarise themselves with the differences between the Regulations and the Act.

Freedom of Information Act Awareness Guidance No 6

Information Reasonably Accessible to the Applicant by Other Means

The right under the Freedom of Information Act to request official information held by public bodies (known as the **right to know**) comes into force in January 2005. The Awareness Guidance series is published by the Information Commissioner to assist public authorities and, in particular, staff who may not have access to specialist advice in thinking about some the issues. The aim is to introduce some of the key concepts in the Act and to suggest the approaches that may be taken in preparing for implementation. Here we look at the exemption from the duty to provide information on request when that information is reasonably accessible to the applicant by other means. The exemption is set out in section 21 of the Act.

A) What does the Act say?

The **right to know** is set out in Section 1 of the Act. In fact, an applicant for information has two related rights. These are:

- the right to be informed whether or not the information requested is held by the authority, and, if so,
- the right to have that information communicated to him.

The Act goes on to make clear that these rights are subject to exemptions and, in section 21, that a public authority does not need to provide information under section 1 of the Act if that information is reasonably accessible to the applicant by other means. It is important to note that s.21, unlike many of the other exemptions in the Act, is not subject to the public interest test: if, as a matter of fact the information requested is accessible to the applicant by other means, then it is exempt.

The thinking behind the exemption is that if there is another route by which someone can obtain information, there is no need for the Act to provide the means of access. Public authorities are under a duty, set out in section 16 of the Act, to "provide advice and assistance, so far as it would be reasonable to expect the authority to do so, to persons who propose to make, or have made requests for information." This means that there should be no possibility of applicants being left in any doubt as to how they can obtain the information which they want.

In the great majority of cases, it will be obvious whether the exemption applies. Occasionally there may be some doubt as to whether the information is genuinely accessible to the particular applicant and whether the authority must therefore do more than simply advise applicants as to how they can obtain the information they want. This guidance looks at the questions which may arise.

B) Cases where payment is required

Applicants may complain that information is not reasonably accessible because it is not free. However, section 21 makes it clear that information may be reasonably accessible to the applicant even though there may be a charge. There are two cases where charges may be made:

- Where there is a specific statutory scheme under which information is provided for a fee, such as information from the local land charges registry.

- Where the information is provided under the authority's publication scheme and the scheme indicates that a charge may be made for information falling within a particular class. (See also the Commissioner's guidance on charging under publication schemes.)

There will, of course, be some cases where the fact that there is a charge for information may mean that it is not reasonably accessible by the applicant. For instance, a public authority may be asked for information contained in its annual report. It may not be reasonable to require the applicant to purchase a copy of the report if the request is only for a small amount of the information contained in it.

C) Disclosures required by law

Section 21 distinguishes between information which an authority or another person is obliged to publish or supply by law and other information. If there is a legal duty to make information available, then it can be considered to be reasonably accessible even though it is not described in a publication scheme. This provision applies even if the information requested is available under statute from another public authority. For instance, a public authority might be asked for information relating to a company which it regulates. If that information is in fact available under statute from Companies House, then it can be considered as reasonably accessible to the applicant.

There is an important exception to this general rule: information which is only available on inspection, for instance by visiting the premises of the authority, is not to be considered reasonably accessible even though it is disclosed or published under statute unless it falls within a class of information included in the authority's publication scheme.

Whether the information is held by the authority itself or a third party, it is important to remember that public authorities are under a duty to assist applicants for information. In this context, this may mean informing them of their rights to obtain information and advising them how to obtain it.

Even though there is no requirement to include information which the authority must disclose under statute within a publication scheme, it will be helpful to do so. Among other things this will be likely to reduce the number of times that the authority has to explain to applicants that the information which they want is in fact available by other means. Similarly, even though a public authority may be within its rights to refer an applicant for information to another authority which has a statutory duty to provide it to the applicant, it will often be as easy for the first authority to provide the information to the applicant as it is to refer him or her to the second authority.

D) Information whose disclosure is not required by law

Where information is not published or made available under statute (other than the FOI Act) but is only available on request from the authority, then it cannot be considered as reasonably accessible unless it falls within a class of information defined in the authority's publication scheme.

It will generally be fair to assume that any information described within a publication scheme and made available under it is reasonably accessible to an applicant and that all the public authority needs to do, therefore, is to draw the applicant's attention to the scheme.

Occasionally this may not be sufficient. The Act does not give public authorities the right to enquire into the circumstances of the applicant. However, if the authority knows or is told of circumstances which will affect the applicant's ability to access the information it should take account of this when handling the request.

a) Travelling and Mobility

If the normal means by which a public authority publishes information is by making it available for inspection but the applicant either lives a considerable distance away or has mobility problems, then the authority should consider providing a hard copy of the information.

(This does not mean that information **must** be provided in hard copy on every occasion that it is requested: simply that the authority should **consider** doing so. A county records office, for instance, whose information may be accessed by visitors, would not normally be expected to photocopy the information which it holds simply because an applicant does not happen to live near by.)

b) Non-English Speakers

If it is clear from the request that the applicant would have difficulty in understanding information in English, it may be reasonable to provide a translation. For instance if the applicant is a member of a local community served by the authority but for which English is not the first language, it may be right to provide a translation in that case. The Act does **not**, however, place a general duty upon public authorities to translate information which it holds into other languages.

c) Disability

Similarly, if an applicant is disabled and requires information in another form, for instance in Braille or on audio tape, then consideration should be given to providing information in the form requested. Again, the Act does not place a duty to provide information in Braille or on audio tape although, as noted above, it should communicate information by the applicant's preferred means if it is "reasonably practicable" to do so.

d) Provision of information in non-electronic form

Publication schemes must specify the manner in which information is published. For many authorities the preferred form of publication is by the web. If this is the only form of publication, then they should provide information in hard copy form to applicants who do not have access to the internet on the basis that the information is not reasonably accessible to the applicant. In such cases, where the authority is not relying upon s.21, it will may be entitled to charge for photocopying and postage in accordance with the Fees Regulations.

E) Considering whether to use the exemption

The question of whether information is reasonably accessible to the applicant by other means is a matter of fact. In deciding to make use of the exemption, public authorities have two choices:

- to make the information available to the applicant outside the framework of the Act (i.e. making it accessible by other means)

- to provide the information according to the normal requirements of the Act

The main consideration is likely to be whether the authority wishes to charge a fee in accordance with the Fees Regulation. This will likely provide that authorities are able to recover the full cost of items such as photocopying and postage. (The Fees Regulation has yet to be finalised.) If it is decided to deal with a request according to the normal requirements of the Act, it will be important to consider section 11. This places a duty on public authorities to communicate information requested by means specified by the applicant if it is "reasonably practicable" to do so.

In deciding whether to charge a fee to some applicants but not to those for whom the information is reasonably accessible by other means, authorities should consider any statutory duties to provide information in other forms. The Welsh Language Act 1993, the Race Relations Act 1976 and the Disability Discrimination Act 1995 may also be relevant.

In addition to statutory requirements, public authorities are also likely to have policies, for instance on the delivery of services for non-English- speaking members of local communities. Giving access to information should be regarded by public authorities as an integral part of their business. Their standards of service delivery should usually complement rather than conflict with their responsibilities under the FOI Act.

F) Key Issues for Implementation

Section 21 is not likely to give rise to many practical difficulties. Generally it will be clear from the nature of the information requested whether it is reasonably accessible to the applicant by other means. The following steps may, however, assist in dealing with any difficulties which may arise.

- Many public authorities already make some information available on request. It is likely to be helpful to distinguish clearly between information published according to a statutory scheme and information made available as a service or on a discretionary basis. If the authority anticipates making use of the s.21 exemption then it should make sure that all non-statutory disclosures fall within classes contained in its publication scheme. There are also good reasons for including statutory disclosures within schemes.

- Authorities making charges for the supply of information should ensure that this is clearly indicated within their schemes. It will often be helpful to include, as a class of information within a publication scheme, a list of documents and other information available at a charge.

- Many public authorities already have policies in place regarding access to information for those with physical disabilities and also as to the provision of information to non-English speakers. It is important that staff with responsibility for responding to FOI requests are fully aware of these policies and able to follow them.

- Authorities may wish to review the means of publication specified in their publication schemes. Where only limited forms of publication (e.g. only electronic) are currently listed, they may wish to describe the alternative means by which information is made available together with any charges that may be made.

F) Further Advice

Further, more detailed advice on some of the issues that arise from this exemption will be published by the Information Commissioner over the course of 2004. In particular, it is intended to publish some advice for the public record offices and archives and on accessibility issues.

Awareness Guidance No 8: Records Management FAQs

The Freedom of Information Act is expected to come fully into force in January 2005. The Act creates a right of access to official information and places a duty on public authorities to publish information in accordance with "publication schemes". In addition, the Act also amends the Public Records Act 1958 and places obligations on public authorities to maintain their records in accordance with the provisions a Code of Practice on Records Management issued by the Lord Chancellor under section 46 of the Act.

The **Awareness Guidance** series is published by the Information Commissioner to assist public authorities and, in particular, staff who may not have access to specialist advice in thinking about some its challenges. The aim is to introduce some of the key concepts in the Act and to suggest the approaches that may be taken in preparing for implementation. Awareness Guidance No 8 takes the form of FAQs on a range of Records Management questions.

General

1. What benefits will good Records Management bring to a Public Authority?

Good records management should be seen as a benefit, not a burden. All organisations (public and private) are advised to have good records management as a key objective in the drive to achieve business efficiency, by ensuring that information is easily retrievable and properly documented. As a natural consequence of this, public authorities will be able to comply more easily with the Modernising Government agenda and other legislation that affects them, the Freedom of Information Act ("the Act") being one example.

It is expected that public authorities will already have good records management in respect of personal information due to the requirements of the Data Protection Act. As such, records management for the Act should be seen as an extension of existing procedures.

2. What is the section 46 Code of Practice?

In accordance with section 46 of the Act, the Lord Chancellor has issued a code of practice which provides guidance to relevant authorities (public authorities and any other office or body whose administrative and departmental records are subject to the Public Records Act) on the practice which, in his opinion, would be desirable for them to follow in connection with the keeping, management and destruction of records.

July 2004 1

3. Does the Code affect all Public Authorities equally?

Part I of the Records Management Code ("the Code") affects all public authorities equally. Part II only applies to Public Record bodies. It is for each public authority to determine how they will meet the requirements of the Code, taking factors such as their own particular size and circumstances into consideration.

4. The Code appears to be a high level document. Has any detailed guidance been issued to assist with compliance?

The National Archives has drawn up detailed model action plans to assist different sectors in meeting the requirements of the Code in time for 2005. Further information can be found at the following link:
http://www.pro.gov.uk/recordsmanagement/access/default.htm

5. Can you afford to leave conformity with the Code until January 2005?

In order for a public authority to respond to a request for information in compliance with the requirements of the Act, it will generally be necessary to have good records management procedures in place and operational. The best way of achieving this is to ensure that information is held and managed in conformity with the Code. This will require forward planning to ensure that this is achieved in time for 1st January 2005.

6. Can poor Records Management lead to a breach of the Act?

Poor records management is not of itself a breach of the Act. However, the Act sets out strict timetables for compliance with a request, ensures that the costs of retrieving information are reasonable and asserts that all recorded information held, wherever it is located within the public authority, is potentially disclosable. If poor records management results in any of these requirements not being met, it will constitute a breach of the Act and the Information Commissioner will be able to consider using his enforcement powers.

7. How will the Information Commissioner (IC) assess good practice?

The IC may, with the consent of the public authority, assess whether that authority has the necessary procedures in place and follows these in accordance with the Code. This may, for instance, be by means of an audit. Alternatively, it may become evident to the IC that a public authority is not complying with the Code on the basis of a complaint(s) submitted by an applicant(s) which relates to their request for information. It is the intention of the IC to publish a paper setting out his approach to audits/inspection later in 2004.

8. What will be the role of the National Archives (TNA) and the Public Record Office of Northern Ireland (PRONI)?

Where the IC considers that a public authority is failing to conform to the Code, he has the authority to issue a Practice Recommendation which will specify the steps which need to be taken in order to achieve such conformity.

Before issuing a Practice Recommendation in relation to records management, the IC may consult with TNA/PRONI, and is required to do so in relation to Public Record bodies. More generally, the IC intends to work with TNA/PRONI in promoting the observance by public authorities of the provisions of the Code. The IC's working relationship with TNA/PRONI will be formalised in a Memorandum of Understanding, which will be in place by 2005.

9. Is there a link between Records Management and Publication Schemes?

In maintaining an effective Publication Scheme, a public authority should already have regard to good practice in records management in relation to information made available by the Scheme. The general right of access under the Act should represent an extension of these procedures to all other recorded information held.

Records Management Training

1. What training should be provided and at what level?

Good records management will not be achieved unless the importance of proper record keeping is impressed upon all staff. This is likely to be achieved for non-specialist staff through induction and top-up training. The extent to which individuals are trained in the requirements of records management can be determined by the nature of their posts.

The Human Resources element of this is covered by a specific section of the Code and in the Model Action Plans devised by the National Archives to assist public authorities in meeting the requirements of the Code.

Records Management Code - Part I

1. What are disposal schedules?

Disposal schedules will form a key element of an organisation's records management policy. They are timetables that set out when individual/groups of records are due for review, transfer to an archives and/or destruction. This will make it easy to establish whether or not a record exists if a request is received. It will also give the public confidence that a public authority has adequate procedures for identifying records that have been requested.

2. Should electronic records be treated any differently to paper-based records?

No. The principles underlying records management – creation, retention, identification, and retrieval of records – apply equally to both electronic and paper records. This means that procedures for e-mail and information held on shared and personal hard drives have to be as robust and detailed as those for other records.

3. What is the status of information held on back-up servers?

Information on a back-up server is not regarded as being held by a public authority for the purposes of the FOI. Such information must have been deleted "twice" in order to claim that it falls outside the scope of the Act:

a) The information should have been sent to the recycle bin, and

b) The information should have been deleted from the recycle bin to the back-up or non-live system

This means that information located in desktop recycle bins would be subject to the Act as this has only been deleted once. On the other hand, information sent to the back-up server is no longer readily retrievable for business purposes, and unscrambling it would be "unreasonable" for the purposes of FOI. When sending information to back-up servers, the intention should be that it is never to be accessed again.

(A paper-based scenario which is analogous to this would be information that is put into a refuse bag and then disposed. Putting the information into the refuse bag would constitute the first deletion and still remain held; sending this information to a refuse site would constitute the second deletion, and at this point no longer be held by the public authority.)

4. What are my obligations if I receive a request for information that is due for destruction?

If the information is contained within a record that is due for destruction within 20 days of the request being received, there is no requirement to release the information. However, it may be worth considering the following points of best practice:

- Delay destruction until disclosure has taken place

- Under the duty to offer advice and assistance, identify whether another authority holds the information, and inform the applicant accordingly.

- Offer to provide similar or related information if this is appropriate.

5. How does the Act apply to records held in remote storage / multi-site organisations?

All information held by a public authority is subject to the Act. No distinction is made between information held by an authority in its head office and in other locations. This means that the procedures and policies on location and retrieval of information will apply in the same way. As such, authorities that operate from several locations and/or have remote storage facilities should apply records management policies consistently throughout the organisation, even if they employ private storage companies. Naturally, for this to be achieved good communications will be essential.

6. Should Environmental Information be managed any differently?

The Environmental Information Regulations and the Act are both access to information regimes, with similar provisions relating to the procedures for dealing with requests. As such, the same principles and policies relating to records management under the Act will apply to Environmental Information. Following the Code of Practice will help you to comply with the Environmental Information Regulations in the same way as they will assist in complying with the Act.

7. What does the Hutton Inquiry tell us about the disclosure of Electronic Records?

Although the Hutton Inquiry will not necessarily become a benchmark for the disclosure of information, it does have a broader significance in terms of the Act by bringing to light the extent to which any electronic information you hold is potentially disclosable. This highlights the importance of good records management with regard to electronic records.

8. How does Records Management under the Act interface with the Data Protection retention and fair processing principles?

The Data Protection Act relates to personal information, whereas the Freedom of Information Act relates to all other recorded information that public authorities hold. As long as you have clearly identified the personal information, these data protection principles are not applicable to the other information that you hold. However, good records management is likely to assist in compliance with the data quality principles, including the requirements that personal data is adequate, relevant and not excessive for the purposes for which it is held, that it is accurate and that it is kept for no longer than is necessary for the purpose for which it is held.

Records Management Code - Part II

1. What is a Public Record Office?

Part II of the Code talks about the review and transfer of Public Records to the appropriate Public Record Office. This is a depository, set up to receive, archive and retain Public Records when they are no longer of use to the organisation which created/held them.

2. What is a Public Record?

Public Records, in general terms, are administrative and departmental records held by Public Record bodies.

3. What is a Public Record Body? Who are they?

A Public Record body is an organisation required by the Public Records Act to transfer public records to the National Archives thirty years after their creation. Broadly speaking, Public Record bodies are central government departments, non-departmental public bodies, the courts, the armed services and the National Health Service.

4. Are there any Public Record Bodies not covered by FOI? (eg Privatised Utilities, Security Services.) What are the implications of this?

Yes. For example, the security and intelligence services, the Courts, and any privatised utilities that hold public records from the pre-privatisation period. This means that these records will only become subject to the Act when they are transferred to the appropriate Public Record Office.

5. What is a Historical Record?

In terms of the Act a record becomes an "historical record" thirty years from the date of its creation. Under the Public Records Act 1958, when a record becomes historical, it must, in most cases, be transferred to the appropriate Public Record Office.

6. How is the 30 year rule affected by FOI?

The standard 30 year closure period for Public Records will disappear when the Act comes fully into force in January 2005. In practice this will mean that when records are transferred they will be considered to be open unless they contain information that is covered by an exemption under the Act. Similarly, with regard to existing records that are either subject to 30 year closure or extended closure, information within them can only be withheld if an exemption under the Act applies. Note that once a record is 30 years old the Act restricts the number of exemptions that can be applied.

7. Files should be closed after 5 years and if further information is required to be put onto it, another should be opened. As such, when does that record become 'historical'?

In these cases the record becomes an 'historical record' 30 years after the creation of the final document. This means that the entire record is considered to be 'created' at the point at which the final document is added.

8. What is the Advisory Council on National Records and Archives? What is its role in extended closure beyond the normal 30 years?

The Advisory Council is appointed to advise the Lord Chancellor on the extended closure of Records under the Public Records Act. If a public authority, when transferring a record to a Public Record Office, wishes for it to remain closed for a period longer than 30 years, this will be referred to the Advisory Council.

When the Act comes fully into force, these duties will be carried out differently. This is because the Advisory Council will only be able to have regard to the exemptions available in the Act in determining whether to accept the restriction of access to all/some of the information.

9. Are electronic records captured by the requirement to transfer records?

All electronic records which constitute departmental records are subject to the requirement to be transferred to a Public Records Office after 30 years, as set out in the Public Records Act 1958 and Part II of the Code, in the same way as their paper-based equivalents.

10. If you hold records on behalf of the Lord Chancellor, what are your obligations?

This is likely to occur where records are transferred to places of deposit other than a Public Record Office, such as local authorities, museums and galleries.

In such circumstances you would be required to operate as if you were a Public Record Office. You would be responsible for dealing requests made under the Act, with two main additional responsibilities:

- If you believe you have a case for extended closure relating to any of this information, you must consult with the Advisory Council (see above), which will provide an appropriate response.

- The authority from which the information originated should be consulted if it attached restrictions to its disclosure. This is in order to assess whether an exemption applies, and if it is a public interest exemption, allow the originating authority to determine whether or not the information should be released.

Additional FAQs specific to Northern Ireland

1. How will the 20 year transfer rule be affected by the Act?

Northern Ireland Public Records are required to be transferred to PRONI when they are 20 years old (unlike Great Britain where the requirement is 30 years). This rule is unaffected by the Act, although the Record will not be considered to be "historical" under the terms of the Act until 30 years have elapsed from the date of its creation. That is the point at which certain exemptions under the Act cease to apply.

2. How does NI Public Record Legislation differ in its coverage?

The Public Records Act (Northern Ireland) 1923 is much wider in its coverage than the equivalent legislation in Great Britain. In addition to Government Departments, NDPBs and the NHS, it extends to all the institutions of Local Government.

3. What is the Northern Ireland equivalent of the Advisory Council?

The Northern Ireland equivalent of the Advisory Council is the "Sensitivity Review Group." Essentially, it fulfils the same role as the Advisory Council, which regulates extended closure. However, it has no statutory basis, is staffed by civil servants, and reports to the appropriate Northern Ireland minister with responsibility for this area.

FREEDOM OF INFORMATION CASEWORK GUIDANCE

Information Commissioner

COURT RECORDS
Section 32 of the Freedom of Information Act 2000

The Information Commissioner has a duty under s.50 of the FOI Act to consider complaints that public authorities have failed to deal properly with requests for information which they receive. The Commissioner also has a more general duty to promote the following of good practice by public authorities and to provide information about the Act to the public.

The most difficult aspect of the Act (and therefore potentially the most controversial) is the application of the exemptions from the *right to know*. These are contained in Part 2 of the Act. As the name suggests, *Casework Guidance,* has been prepared primarily for use by complaints resolution staff in the Information Commissioner's Office. The guidance attempts to provide and interpretation of the various exemptions, to give some indication of the Commissioner's general approach, and, where appropriate, to describe the kinds of issues that are likely to come to the fore when the exemptions and the public interest test are applied.

Although the primary audience is internal, the Commissioner recognises that public authorities and members of the public will have an interest in understanding his point of view. For that reason he has decided to publish this internal guidance.

It is important to note that this is living guidance. It will be revised and supplemented in the light of cases considered from January 2005. Moreover, although not intended to be a formal external consultation, the Commissioner welcomes comments and suggestions on the guidance as it currently stands.

A) THE EXEMPTION

"32 –   (1) Information held by a public authority is exempt information if it is held only by virtue of being contained in -
   (a) any document filed with, or otherwise placed in the custody of, a court for the purposes of proceedings in a particular cause or matter,
   (b) any document served upon, or by, a public authority for the purposes if proceedings in a particular cause or matter, or
   (c) any document created by-
      (i) a court, or
      (ii) a member of the administrative staff of a court, for the purposes of proceedings in a particular cause or matter.'

(2) Information held by a public authority is exempt information if it is held only by virtue of being contained in –
(a) any document placed in the custody of a person conducting an inquiry or arbitration, for the purposes of the inquiry or arbitration, or
 (b) any document created by a person conducting an inquiry or arbitration, for the purposes of the inquiry or arbitration.'

FOI CASEWORK GUIDANCE   1   **COURT RECORDS**

V1.0 (13/07/0)4

FREEDOM OF INFORMATION CASEWORK GUIDANCE

(3) The duty to confirm or deny does not arise in relation to information which is (or if it were held by the public authority would be) exempt information by virtue of this section.

(4) In this section –
(a) "court" includes any tribunal or body exercising the judicial power of the State,
(b) "proceedings in a particular cause or matter" includes any inquest or post-mortem examination,
(c) "inquiry" means any inquiry or hearing held under any provision contained in, or made under, an enactment, and
(d) except in relation to Scotland, "arbitration" means any arbitration to which Part 1 of the Arbitration Act 1996 applies."

B) MEANING AND GENERAL EFFECT

Section 2 of the Act explains that this is an absolute exemption. In other words, unlike many other exemptions in the Act it is not subject to a public interest test. If information requested falls within the scope of the exemption there is neither a duty to confirm or deny that the information is held nor to communicate the information to the applicant. After 30 years (see "Shelf life of the exemption" – below) the exemption ceases to have effect.

The exemption applies if a document has been:

- filed with or otherwise placed in the custody of a court, or
- served upon or by a public authority, for the purposes of court proceedings, or
- placed in the custody of a person conducting an inquiry or arbitration or the purposes of that inquiry or arbitration, or
- created by a court or member of the administrative staff for the purposes of court proceedings, or
- created by a person conducting an inquiry or arbitration for the purposes of that inquiry or arbitration

In other words for this exemption to apply a court case, inquiry, or arbitration must have taken place or currently be taking place. If, for example, court proceedings are being contemplated but have not yet been commenced, this exemption will not apply to a draft document (for example an originating application) prepared in advance of proceedings actually being issued. However, in these circumstances other exemptions may apply.

a) Purpose of the exemption

The exemption is unusual in that it seeks not to protect the information which is covered in itself but rather to exempt from disclosure the fact that the information is contained in a court record or a document held for the purposes of an enquiry or arbitration.

FREEDOM OF INFORMATION CASEWORK GUIDANCE

For instance, a public authority involved in litigation regarding a written agreement will have a copy of that agreement. A request for information about the agreement will not be exempt just because the information is also contained in the authority's statement of case. However if a request were made for the information contained in the authority's statement of case, the exemption would apply since to respond would be to disclose the basis of the litigation.

In this example, it would not be possible to use the Act to ask if the agreement was held as part of the court record and, having discovered this, to make a second request for a copy of the original records since sub-section (3) makes clear that there is no duty to confirm or deny the existence of information held as part of a court record or for the purposes of an inquiry or arbitration.

b) Shelf life of the exemption

For records less than 30 years old, this is an absolute exemption. If the information requested falls within the exemption, there is neither a duty to confirm or deny that information is held, nor to communicate the information to the applicant. After 30 years, court and arbitration records and those of inquiries become "historical" information and are no longer protected by the exemption. Where a set of documents forming a record covered by the exemption were created at different times, the 30 years starts from the day on which the last of the documents was created.

c) Who may be able to claim the exemption

Courts and public inquiries are not public authorities for the purpose of the Act. This means that documents produced by administrative staff of the courts such as court listings (the schedules of the daily proceedings in courts) are not accessible under the Act since the staff are in fact acting on behalf of the Judge. (It may be that this information is available by other means, see "Other means of accessing court information" – below.)

Courts and inquiries may be the responsibility public authorities such as government departments and local authorities. These bodies are, of course, subject to the Act although it is unlikely that this will mean that they will hold any documents falling within the scope of the exemption.

Public authorities such as the Legal Services Ombudsman, police and the Legal Services Commission are more likely to hold such documents, as indeed may public authorities who are parties to litigation.

d) Existing access rules

The effect of the exemption is to leave intact the existing rules regarding access to/publication of information contained in court records or held for the purposes of enquiries or arbitration. These rules have been developed to ensure the right to a fair trial including the presumption of innocence. Broadly speaking, the effect of the rules is that a party to proceedings will have rights of access to information under the normal disclosure rules. Third parties, including the press, will have access to

FREEDOM OF INFORMATION CASEWORK GUIDANCE

information which is made public in open court (and conversely no access to information which is subject to proceedings *in camera.*)

(See also under "Other Means of Accessing Court Information" below.)

e) What s.32 cannot be used for

This exemption cannot be used to refuse to confirm the existence of court proceedings or anything relating to litigation (or indeed of the existence of an inquiry or arbitration). Either the legal professional privilege exemption or the laws of contempt should provide adequate protection against any harmful disclosure.

C) COURT RECORDS

Subsection (1) is concerned with court records. A court record contains documents created for a "particular cause or matter" (i.e. case). The information most likely to fall within the exemption will be either information known to a public authority because it is contained in documents served on it by another party in litigation (the taking of legal action); or information held by the public authority which was recorded only in connection with the litigation.

a) Examples of information falling within the exemption

These include such documents such as witness statements, statement of case such as particulars of claim, defence, counterclaim, defence to counterclaim and reply, and details of when and how a fine is paid. Other types of documents forming part of the court record include a warrant issued by a magistrate at his home, indictment (charge) sheet and bail application sheets.

b) Examples on information falling outside the exemption

In deciding whether the exemption applies, it may be equally important to think about the documents which would not constitute court records. For example, a court record would not include government information concerning persistent youth offenders. This information would not have been created for the particular cause or matter in hand.

c) Information which **may** fall within the exemption

Other documents such as exhibits may temporarily form part of court records having been placed in the custody of a court for the purpose of a particular cause or matter but subsequently be returned at the direction of a judge to the appropriate party. An example might be a set of business accounts or a birth certificate. While the documents are in the possession of the court they form part of the court record. If they have been returned to a public authority, they may be accessible from the authority under FOI. However, any record of the document having been lodged with the court would be exempt.

(For other examples of court records and information contained in them see the Court Services website.)

d) Inadmissible evidence

If evidence is deemed inadmissible it will not be considered as part of a court record. If this occurs before the case actually gets to court the inadmissible evidence will either be removed from the case notes or stay in the notes with a line drawn through it. Whatever happens, the document will not be part of the court record and therefore will not be exempt. If, during a case the judge rules evidence inadmissible it will be removed and returned to the appropriate party. Again it will not form part of the court record and will therefore not be exempt.

e) Other means of accessing court information

During the course of a trial, members of the public is often able to inspect documents presented to the court (although a court will normally refuse to allow this if it would compromise the interests of justice or the public interest, would reveal medical or other confidential information or would adversely affect the interests of children.)

A hearing can be held in public or in private (*in camera*). If it is held in public members of the public can obtain a copy of a judgement or an order made but will have to pay a fee. If the hearing is held in private a member of the public who is not a party to the proceedings has to seek leave of the judge who gave the judgement or made the order.

f) Copies of documents

An original document held as part of a court record will be exempt; however any copies of the document may or may not be.

If the original document was:

- filed with or placed in the custody of a court for the purposes of proceedings in a particular cause or matter or
- served upon, or by, a public authority for the purposes of proceedings in a particular cause or matter or
- created by a court or any member of the administrative staff of a court

then the copy will be exempt under s.32 (for example a copy of a particulars of claim in civil proceedings). However if a copy of the document was made **before** any proceedings were considered then the copy would not be exempt.

For example if a public authority was involved in litigation over a contract they would have both the original contract and a copy of it. The original contract will be given to the court and become part of the court record but the copy will be kept by the public authority. As the copy would have been made **before** there was any question of proceedings, it would not be exempt under s32.

FREEDOM OF INFORMATION CASEWORK GUIDANCE

g) Storage

Courts records will not necessarily be held by the courts themselves. At present, court records can be kept by either the magistrates' courts committee or the courts services (which deals with the higher courts). The magistrates' courts committee instructs its chief executive officer to keep the records whereas it is the duty of the court services department itself to keep any court records allocated to them.

D) INQUIRIES

For information held for the purpose of an inquiry to fall within this exemption, the inquiry must be governed by a statute and have the powers to compel the production of documents, evidence and/or compel witnesses to attend. The information in question might be contained in any document given to a person conducting a specific inquiry or nformation in any document created by a person conducting a specific inquiry. In order to help decide if an inquiry falls under this exemption or not, it may often be useful to look at the status of the inquiry and the terms of reference of an inquiry. These specify the circumstances under which the inquiry was set up and what powers it has.

a) Examples of statutory inquiries

- Central Government Inquiry: The Public Inquiry into Paediatric Cardiac Surgery Services at Bristol Royal Infirmary. This was set up under the National Health Service Act 1977 which also provided powers to compel both the production of documents and witnesses.

- Local Government Inquiry: The Local Authority Social Services Act 1970 s7C (Inquiries) allows the Secretary of State to order an inquiry into how a local authority exercises its social services functions.

b) Non-statutory inquiries which may fall within the exemption

Some non-statutory inquiries may fall under s32. Under s.17A of the Coroners Act 1988 (as amended by the Access to Justice 1999), coroners are required to adjourn an inquest if a public inquiry can 'fulfil the function of the inquest'. S.17A applies where a public inquiry is conducted or chaired by a judge and the Lord Chancellor is satisfied that the cause of death is likely to be adequately investigated by the inquiry. Examples include:

- The inquiry over the Ladbroke Road rail crash
- The inquiry into Dr Harold Shipman

Where the exemption is claimed in relation to information held in connection with non-statutory inquiries, it will be particularly important to ascertain the precise basis of the inquiry.

c) Examples of enquiries falling outside the exemption

FREEDOM OF INFORMATION CASEWORK GUIDANCE

It may also be helpful to think about the sorts of inquiry whose information will **not** fall within the exemption. Examples include:

- Central Government Inquiry: The Independent Inquiry into Inequalities in Health was not set up under any statute (it was requested by a minister). Furthermore it had no powers to compel evidence or witnesses.

- Local Government Inquiry: A local authority ad hoc inquiry is set up for a specific reason. It is not governed by a statutory or procedural code and can include serious complaints against an authority or failures in its services or administration.

FREEDOM OF INFORMATION CASEWORK GUIDANCE

E) ARBITRATION

Arbitration is the settling of a dispute by a third party (arbitrator) whose decision is based on the rules of English law. It is a voluntary process which both parties must sign up to. Once they do they are bound by the arbitrator's decision (known as the award) which is final and has the same effect as a court judgment.

Part 1(1) of the Arbitration Act 1996 provides:

(a) *the object of arbitration is to obtain the fair resolution of disputes by an impartial tribunal without unnecessary delay or expense;*
(b) *the parties should be free to agree how their disputes are resolved, subject only to such safeguards as are necessary in the public interest;*
(c) *in matters governed by this Part the court should not intervene except as provided by this Part*

a) When Part 1 of the Arbitration Act 1996 applies

The most important point to consider when deciding if arbitration falls under the Arbitration Act 1996 Part 1 is whether there is a written arbitration agreement. If there is no written arbitration agreement, Part 1 does not apply.

b) Arbitration Agreement

This is a written agreement which refers a dispute to arbitration and should include: the name and place where the arbitration will take place, appointment of the arbitrator(s) or how they will be appointed if the two parties cannot agree and the procedure for appointing an umpire if two arbitrators are involved and cannot agree.

An arbitration agreement will be deemed to be in writing if:

- the agreement is in writing even if it is not signed by the parties;
- the agreement is made by exchanging communications in writing or;
- the agreement is evidenced in writing (this is where the parties do not agree in writing to go to arbitration but the agreement is recorded by one of the parties or by a third party agreed on by both parties)

Part 1 applies to arbitration that began on or after 31 January 1997, under an arbitration agreement in England, Northern Ireland or Wales. It also applies to all arbitration under an enactment (statutory arbitration) whether the enactment was passed before or after 31 January 1997 except where the application of Part 1 is:

- inconsistent with any enactment/authorised rules/procedures concerned or;
- excluded by any other enactment

c) Examples of arbitration that fall within s.32

Statutory arbitration (please note that sections 85-87 and 92-98 of Part II of the Arbitration Act also apply to Part I) and employment disputes.

d) Examples of arbitration that fall outside s.32

Consumer arbitration agreements which falls under Part II of the Arbitration Act 1996.

F) GLOSSARY

a) Section32 (4)

Some of the phrases used in this section of the Act are defined in sub-section 4 as follows:

s.32 (4) (a) states: ' *"court" includes any tribunal or body exercising the judicial power of the State.'*

'Court' – this is the same interpretation as s19 Contempt of Court Act 1981

'Tribunal' is a group of people made up of a chairman (usually a barrister/solicitor) and others who exercise a judicial function to determine matters relating to specific interests e.g. VAT tribunals (appeals against the level of duty levied by HM Customs and Excise).

s.32 (4) (b) states: ' *"proceedings in a particular cause or matter" includes any inquest or post-mortem examination.'*

'proceedings' are the conducting of business before a court
'cause' – a court action
matter' – proceedings commenced under an 'originating application'. This is a method of starting proceedings under the authority of a specific act of Parliament where the applicant asks the Court to grant an order in their favour
'inquest' – an inquiry in to a sudden death whose cause is unknown held by a coroner (Coroners Act 1988) who is a qualified barrister/solicitor/medical practitioner with at least 5 years experience

A post-mortem, sometimes referred to as an "autopsy" is the examination of a body after death to try and establish the cause of death. Post-mortems are often requested by coroners.

FREEDOM OF INFORMATION CASEWORK GUIDANCE

(c) *"inquiry" means any inquiry or hearing held under any provision contained in, or made under, an enactment*

'Hearing' – the action or process of listening to evidence etc in a court of law or before an official.

s.32 (4) (d) defines Arbitration (see above).

b) Other Terms

The section also uses a number of terms which are undefined and which should therefore be given their normal interpretation. These include:

'A member of the administrative staff of a court' – this does not cover judges or magistrates as they are 'judicial appointments' and pass any documents they create to a Magistrates' Court Committee or the Court Services. However, all other staff concerned with a court are considered administrative staff. This includes, for example, security guards who bring prisoners to court and record the time of arrival and departure of an accused. This note will be considered a court record because it is created for a particular cause or matter and would therefore fall under this exemption.

'Any document' – this includes everything that is generated for or filed with the court, for a particular cause or matter. However trial bundles would not be considered as part of a court record even though they are produced for a particular court case. This is because they are considered a 'road map' to a case and will contain copies of documents already in the case notes.

'Document' – something that records/transmits information (typically in writing on paper). Documents used as evidence in court include: books, maps, plans, drawings, photographs, graphs, discs, tapes, films.

'Filed with' – delivered to the court office by post or other means. The information does not have to be given to anybody just delivered to the court office.

'Only by virtue of' – this deals with the fact that the information contained in the document is exempt only because it is in that particular document.

G) TYPES OF COURT RECORD

The following are examples of commonly used 'court records'. This list is not definitive therefore before deciding whether a document is a 'court record' the document should be examined.

FREEDOM OF INFORMATION CASEWORK GUIDANCE

a) Criminal cases

Witness statements
Bail application forms
Pre-sentence reports
Skeleton arguments
Plea-in-mitigation

b) Civil cases

Acknowledgment of service
Admission Appellant's
Notice Application for an injunction
Certificate of Judgment
Certificate of service Claim form - Part 7, Probate Claim, for possession of property
for relief against forfeiture, accelerated possession procedure, arbitration, Part 8,
Part 20
Defence form
Defence/counterclaim
Listing questionnaire - pre-trial checklist
Notice of payment into court - under order part 37 or part 36
Particulars of claim
Respondent's Notice
Skeleton arguments
Statement of Costs

Freedom of Information

Factsheet

Information Commissioner
Promoting public access to official information
and protecting your personal information

What does it mean for you?

The right under the **Freedom of Information Act** (the Act) and the **Environmental Information Regulations** (EIR) to request information held by public authorities, known as the **right to know**, comes into force from January 2005. The Act and the EIR allow you to access recorded information (such as e-mails, meeting minutes, research or reports) held by public authorities in England, Northern Ireland and Wales. Under the Act, a public authority includes:

- Central government and government departments
- Local authorities
- Hospitals, doctors' surgeries, dentists, pharmacists and opticians
- State schools, colleges and universities
- Police forces and prison services

The role of the **Information Commissioner's Office** (ICO) is to enforce and promote the Act and the EIR. It has responsibility for ensuring that information is disclosed promptly and that exemptions from disclosure are applied lawfully.

What is an exemption and how does it work?

Some information could be exempt from disclosure. There are 23 **exemptions** in the Act, some of which are **'absolute'** and some **'qualified'**, and 12 **exceptions** from disclosure in the EIR, all of which are qualified.

- Where information falls under an **absolute exemption**, the harm to the public interest that would result from its disclosure is already established, for example, in relation to personal information, or if disclosure would result in an actionable breach of confidence.

- If a public authority believes that the information is covered by a **qualified exemption** or **exception** it must apply the public interest test.

What is the public interest test?

The public interest test favours disclosure where a qualified exemption or an exception applies. In such cases, the information may be withheld only if the public authority considers that the public interest in withholding the information is greater than the public interest in disclosing it.

How do I make a request?

- Make the information as specific as possible. If your request is too broad the public authority may ask you to clarify it. This could mean it takes longer to get the information.
- Provide as full a description as possible of the information you require.
- Be clear about the format you would prefer to receive the information in, for example, by e-mail or as a paper copy.

1

What happens once my request has been received?

Any request for information should be treated by the public authority as a formal request for information and we suggest that e-mails or letters are clearly marked as freedom of information or Environmental Information Regulations requests to avoid any confusion. Under the EIR, verbal requests must be treated as formal requests for information.

- Public authorities must respond promptly to requests or, in any event, within 20 working days although under freedom of information they have longer to consider whether the disclosure of normally exempt information would be in the public interest.

- There is no extension to the time limit for considering the public interest test under Environmental Information Regulations, except where the request is complex and voluminous.

- When considering the public interest test, the public authority must do so 'within a reasonable time.'

What if the information is refused?

Where a public authority decides not to disclose the information requested it must give reasons for its decision, it must explain how the exemption or exception applies and it must explain the arguments under the public interest test. Under the Environmental Information Regulations the public authority must reconsider its decision and reconsideration is also recommended for refusals under freedom of information. The public authority must also inform you of your right to complain to the ICO.

How can the ICO help and what is the legal process?

- You may apply to the ICO for a decision about whether the request has been dealt with according to the Act or the EIR if, for example, you believe there has been excessive delay or if you wish to dispute the application of an exemption or refusals made on public interest grounds.

- The ICO may serve a decision notice on the public authority either confirming the decision made by the public authority or directing it to disclose information within a certain time.

- Non-compliance with a decision notice may constitute contempt of court.

- If you or the public authority disagrees with the ICO's decision you have 28 days to appeal to the independent **Information Tribunal.**

- The Information Tribunal may uphold the ICO's decision notice, amend it (for example change the time frame for release of information) or overturn it. Non-compliance with the Information Tribunal's notice may also constitute contempt of court.

Additional Information

Additional guidance on the Freedom of Information Act and the Environmental Information Regulations are available on our website at www.informationcommissioner.gov.uk

To contact our helpline please telephone 01625 545545.

To contact our press office please telephone 020 7282 2960.

Other specially commissioned reports

The commercial exploitation of intellectual property rights by licensing

CHARLES DESFORGES   £125

1 85418 285 4 • 2001

Expert advice and techniques for the identification and successful exploitation of key opportunities.

This report will show you:

* how to identify and secure profitable opportunities
* strategies and techniques for negotiating the best agreement
* the techniques of successfully managing a license operation.

Damages and other remedies for breach of commercial contracts

ROBERT RIBEIRO   £125

1 85418 226 X • 2002

This valuable new report sets out a systematic approach for assessing the remedies available for various types of breach of contract, what the remedies mean in terms of compensation and how the compensation is calculated.

Commercial contracts – drafting techniques and precedents

ROBERT RIBEIRO   £125

1 85418 210 2 • 2002

The Report will:

* Improve your commercial awareness and planning skills
* Enhance your legal foresight and vision
* Help you appreciate the relevance of rules and guidelines set out by the courts
* Ensure you achieve your or your client's commercial objectives

The Competition Act 1998: practical advice and guidance

SUSAN SINGLETON   £149

1 85418 205 6 • 2001

Failure to operate within UK and EU competition rules can lead to heavy fines of up to 10 per cent of a business's total UK turnover.

Insights into successfully managing the in-house legal function

BARRY O'MEARA   £65

1 85418 174 2 • 2000

Negotiating the fault line between private practice and in-house employment can be tricky, as the scope for conflicts of interest is greatly increased. *Insights into successfully managing the In-house legal function* discusses and suggests ways of dealing with these and other issues.

For full details of any title, and to view sample extracts please visit: www.thorogood.ws

You can place an order in four ways:

1 **Email**: orders@thorogood.ws
2 **Telephone**: +44 (0)20 7749 4748
3 **Fax**: +44 (0)20 7729 6110
4 **Post**: Thorogood, 10-12 Rivington Street, London EC2A 3DU, UK

The legal protection of databases

SIMON CHALTON   £145

1 85418 245 5 • 2001

Inventions can be patented, knowledge can be protected, but what of information itself?

This valuable report examines the current EU [and so EEA] law on the legal protection of databases, including the *sui generis* right established when the European Union adopted its Directive 96/9/EC in 1996.

Litigation costs

MICHAEL BACON   £95

1 85418 241 2 • 2001

The rules and regulations are complex – but can be turned to advantage.

The astute practitioner will understand the importance and relevance of costs to the litigation process and will wish to learn how to turn the large number of rules to maximum advantage.

Tendering and negotiating for MoD contracts

TIM BOYCE   £125

1 85418 276 5 • 2002

This specially commissioned report aims to draw out the main principles, processes and procedures involved in tendering and negotiating MoD contracts.

International commercial agreements

REBECCA ATTREE   £175

1 85418 286 2 • 2002

A major new report on recent changes to the law and their commercial implications and possibilities.

The report explains the principles and techniques of successful international negotiation and provides a valuable insight into the commercial points to be considered as a result of the laws relating to: pre-contract, private international law, resolving disputes (including alternative methods, such as mediation), competition law, drafting common clauses and contracting electronically.

It also examines in more detail certain specific international commercial agreements, namely agency and distribution and licensing.

Email – legal issues

SUSAN SINGLETON   £129

1 85418 215 3 • 2001

What are the chances of either you or your employees breaking the law?

The report explains clearly:

- How to establish a sensible policy and whether or not you are entitled to insist on it as binding
- The degree to which you may lawfully monitor your employees' e-mail and Internet use
- The implications of the Regulation of Investigatory Powers Act 2000 and the Electronic Communications Act 2000
- How the Data Protection Act 1998 affects the degree to which you can monitor your staff
- What you need to watch for in the Human Rights Act 1998
- TUC guidelines
- Example of an e-mail and Internet policy document.

For full details of any title, and to view sample extracts please visit: www.thorogood.ws

You can place an order in four ways:

1   **Email:** orders@thorogood.ws
2   **Telephone:** +44 (0)20 7749 4748
3   **Fax:** +44 (0)20 7729 6110
4   **Post:** Thorogood, 10-12 Rivington Street, London EC2A 3DU, UK

Employee sickness and fitness for work – successfully dealing with the legal system

GILLIAN HOWARD   £129

1 85418 281 1 • 2002

Many executives see Employment Law as an obstacle course or, even worse, an opponent – but it can contribute positively to keeping employees fit and productive.

This specially commissioned report will show you how to get the best out of your employees, from recruitment to retirement, while protecting yourself and your firm to the full.

Data protection law for employers

SUSAN SINGLETON   £129

1 85418 283 8 • 2003

The new four-part Code of Practice under the Data Protection Act 1998 on employment and data protection makes places a further burden of responsibility on employers and their advisers. The Data protection Act also applies to manual data, not just computer data, and a new tough enforcement policy was announced in October 2002.

Successful graduate recruitment

JEAN BRADING   £69

1 85418 270 6 • 2001

Practical advice on how to attract *and* keep the best.

Successfully defending employment tribunal cases

DENNIS HUNT   £95

1 85418 267 6 • 2003

Fully up to date with all the Employment Act 2002 changes.

165,000 claims were made last year and the numbers are rising. What will you do when one comes your way?

How to turn your HR strategy into reality

TONY GRUNDY   £129

1 85418 183 1 • 1999

A practical guide to developing and implementing an effective HR strategy.

Internal communications

JAMES FARRANT   £129

1 85418 149 1 • 2003

How to improve your organisation's internal communications – and performance as a result.

There is growing evidence that the organisations that 'get it right' reap dividends in corporate energy and enhanced performance.

Mergers and acquisitions – confronting the organisation and people issues

MARK THOMAS   £95

1 85418 008 8 • 1997

Why do so many mergers and acquisitions end in tears and reduced shareholder value?

This report will help you to understand the key practical and legal issues, achieve consensus and involvement at all levels, understand and implement TUPE regulations and identify the documentation that needs to be drafted or reviewed.

New ways of working

STEPHEN JUPP   £99

1 85418 169 6 • 2000

New ways of working examines the nature of the work done in an organisation and seeks to *optimise the working practices and the whole context* in which the work takes place.

A practical guide to knowledge management

SUE BRELADE, CHRISTOPHER HARMAN   £69

1 85418 230 7 • 2003

Managing knowledge in companies is nothing new. However, the development of a *separate discipline* called 'knowledge management' *is* new – the introduction of recognised techniques and approaches for effectively managing the knowledge resources of an organisation. This report will provide you with these techniques.

Reviewing and changing contracts of employment

ANNELISE PHILLIPS, TOM PLAYER and PAULA ROME   £129

1 85418 296 X • 2003

The Employment Act 2002 has raised the stakes. Imperfect understanding of the law and poor drafting will now be very costly.

This new report will:

* Ensure that you have a total grip on what should be in a contract and what should not

* Explain step by step how to achieve changes in the contract of employment without causing problems

* Enable you to protect clients' sensitive business information

* Enhance your understanding of potential conflict areas and your ability to manage disputes effectively.

Email – legal issues

SUSAN SINGLETON   £129

1 85418 215 3 • 2001

What are the chances of either you or your employees breaking the law?

The report explains clearly:

* How to establish a sensible policy and whether or not you are entitled to insist on it as binding

* The degree to which you may lawfully monitor your employees' e-mail and Internet use

* The implications of the Regulation of Investigatory Powers Act 2000 and the Electronic Communications Act 2000

* How the Data Protection Act 1998 affects the degree to which you can monitor your staff

* What you need to watch for in the Human Rights Act 1998

* TUC guidelines

* Example of an e-mail and Internet policy document.

Applying the Employment Act 2002 – crucial developments for employers and employees

AUDREY WILLIAMS   £129

1 85418 253 6 • 2003

The Act represents a major shift in the commercial environment, with far-reaching changes for employers and employees. The majority of the new rights under the family friendly section take effect from April 2003 with most of the other provisions later in the year.

The consequences of getting it wrong, for both employer and employee, will be considerable – financial and otherwise. The Act affects nearly every aspect of the work place, including:

* flexible working

* family rights (adoption, paternity and improved maternity leave)

* changes to internal disciplinary and grievance procedures

* significant changes to unfair dismissal legislation

* new rights for those employed on fixed-term contracts

* the introduction of new rights for learning representatives from an employer's trade union

This specially commissioned new report examines each of the key developments where the Act changes existing provisions or introduces new rights. Each chapter deals with a discreet area.

Implementing an integrated marketing communications strategy

NORMAN HART   £99

1 85418 120 3 • 1999

Just what is meant by marketing communications, or 'marcom'? How does it fit in with other corporate functions, and in particular how does it relate to business and marketing objectives?

Strategic customer planning

ALAN MELKMAN AND
PROFESSOR KEN SIMMONDS   £95

1 85418 255 2 • 2001

This is very much a 'how to' Report. After reading those parts that are relevant to your business, you will be able to compile a plan that will work within your particular organisation for you, a powerful customer plan that you can implement immediately. Charts, checklists and diagrams throughout.

Corporate community investment

CHRIS GENASI   £75

1 85418 192 0 • 1999

Supporting good causes is big business – and good business. Corporate community investment (CCI) is the general term for companies' support of good causes, and is a very fast growing area of PR and marketing.

Defending your reputation

SIMON TAYLOR   £95

1 85418 251 • 2001

'Buildings can be rebuilt, IT systems replaced. People can be recruited, but a reputation lost can never be regained...'

'The media will publish a story – you may as well ensure it is your story'   *Simon Taylor*

'News is whatever someone, somewhere, does not want published'   *William Randoplh Hearst*

When a major crisis does suddenly break, how ready will you be to defend your reputation?

Insights into understanding the financial media – an insider's view

SIMON SCOTT   £99

1 85418 083 5 • 1998

This practical briefing will help you understand the way the financial print and broadcast media works in the UK.

European lobbying guide

BRYAN CASSIDY   £129

1 85418 144 0 • 2000

Understand how the EU works and how to get your message across effectively to the right people.

Lobbying and the media: working with politicians and journalists

MICHAEL BURRELL   £95

1 85418 240 4 • 2001

Lobbying is an art form rather than a science, so there is inevitably an element of judgement in what line to take. This expert report explains the knowledge and techniques required.

Strategic planning in public relations

KIERAN KNIGHTS   £69

1 85418 225 0 • 2001

Tips and techniques to aid you in a new approach to campaign planning.

Strategic planning is a fresh approach to PR. An approach that is *fact-based* and scientific, clearly presenting the arguments for a campaign proposal backed with *evidence*.

Managing corporate reputation – the new currency

SUSAN CROFT and JOHN DALTON   £125

1 85418 272 2 • 2003

ENRON, WORLDCOM... who next?

At a time when trust in corporations has plumbed new depths, knowing how to manage corporate reputation professionally and effectively has never been more crucial.

Surviving a corporate crisis – 100 things you need to know

PAUL BATCHELOR   £125

1 85418 208 0 • 2003

Seven out of ten organisations that experience a corporate crisis go out of business within 18 months.

This very timely report not only covers remedial action after the event but offers expert advice on preparing every department and every key player of the organisation so that, should a crisis occur, damage of every kind is limited as far as possible.

FINANCE

Tax aspects of buying and selling companies

MARTYN INGLES   £99

1 85418 189 0 • 2001

This report takes you through the buying and selling process *from the tax angle*. It uses straightforward case studies to highlight the issues and more important strategies that are likely to have a significant impact on the taxation position.

Tax planning opportunities for family businesses in the new regime

CHRISTOPHER JONES   £49

1 85418 154 8 • 2000

Following recent legislative and case law changes, the whole area of tax planning for family businesses requires very careful and thorough attention in order to avoid the many pitfalls.

Practical techniques for effective project investment appraisal

RALPH TIFFIN   £99

1 85418 099 1 • 1999

How to ensure you have a reliable system in place.

Spending money on projects automatically necessitates an effective appraisal system – a way of deciding whether the correct decisions on investment have been made.

Strategy implementation through project management

TONY GRUNDY   £95

1 85418 250 1 • 2001

The gap

Far too few managers know how to apply project management techniques to their strategic planning. The result is often strategy that is poorly thought out and executed.

The answer

Strategic project management is a new and powerful process designed to manage complex projects by combining traditional business analysis with project management techniques.

High performance leadership

PUBLISHED BY CRF PUBLISHING IN ASSOCIATION WITH THOROGOOD   £282

0 95443 900 7 • 2003

A major new report combining solid research, case studies and contributions from expert thinkers. This 234 page report analyses contemporary leadership for success, failure and derailment. It examines what leaders and leadership enablers – HR/OD directors/VPs who have to plan, deploy or build leadership – must do. And it makes challenging recommendations.

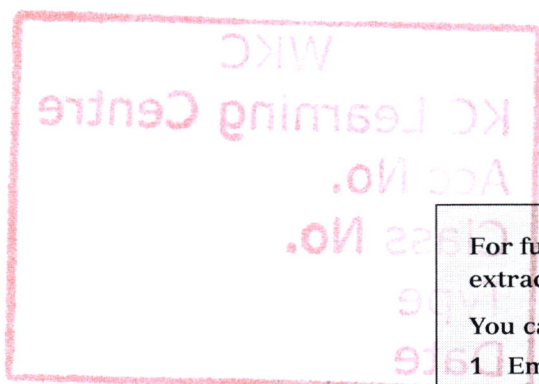

For full details of any title, and to view sample extracts please visit: www.thorogood.ws

You can place an order in four ways:

1 **Email**: orders@thorogood.ws
2 **Telephone**: +44 (0)20 7749 4748
3 **Fax**: +44 (0)20 7729 6110
4 **Post**: Thorogood, 10-12 Rivington Street, London EC2A 3DU, UK